SHE READS TRUTH

THIS BOOK BELONGS TO

START DATE

| MONTH | DAY | YEAR |

SHE READS TRUTH™

© 2017 She Reads Truth, LLC
All rights reserved.

ISBN 978-1-946282-30-9

Unless otherwise noted, all Scripture is taken from the Christian Standard
Bible®, Copyright © 2017 by Holman Bible Publishers. Used by permission.
Christian Standard Bible® and CSB® are federally registered trademarks of
Holman Bible Publishers.

Scripture quotations marked ESV are from ESV® Bible (The Holy Bible,
English Standard Version®), copyright © 2001 by Crossway, a publishing
ministry of Good News Publishers. Used by permission. All rights reserved.

Joy to the World

SHE READS TRUTH

Nashville, Tennessee

Let the whole earth shout to the LORD;
be jubilant, shout for joy, and sing.

PSALM 98:4

Advent starts early at our office. In fact, the "advent" of Advent at She Reads Truth begins with Christmas lights and candles in the conference room in July.

One early meeting we sat together to brainstorm titles for this plan. Last year, it was *Born Is the King*, and the year before that, *Christ Was Born for This*. Our tradition is to use a Christmas carol lyric for the title, which puts a fun amount of pressure on the team to come up with the best obscure-yet-recognizable line to name our most beloved plan of the year.

Our content director, Russ, had his heart set on "What Child is This?" and I was angling for some lyrics from "O Holy Night." But Amanda quietly sat back with a smile on her face. After everyone finished making their cases, she offered hers— "Joy to the World." She went on to tell us how the song was Isaac Watts' New Testament response to Psalm 98.

"Joy to the World" is the perfect Advent song because it reminds us why we celebrate Christmas. We are rejoicing in the birth of our King who rules with righteousness, who sets us free from sin and death, and who will reign forever with grace and truth.

Our hope as we assembled this Advent reading plan was to go back to the basics—to read the traditional messianic prophecies, to see them fulfilled in Christ, and to walk through the nativity narrative that is the centerpiece of it all.

So read the story of your salvation and be glad. Savor the words you read, the recipes you prepare, and the prayers you pray. Sit long in this season of remembrance and anticipation, then rise to sing a song of celebration.

Joy to the world! The Lord has come. Let earth receive her King.

Merry Christmas!

Raechel & Amanda

Raechel Myers and Amanda Bible Williams
EDITORS-IN-CHIEF

For to us a child is born,
to us a son is given;
and the government shall
be upon his shoulder,
and his name shall be called
Wonderful Counselor,
Mighty God,
Everlasting Father,
Prince of Peace.

What Is Advent?

Advent is a Latin word that means "coming."

The season of Advent in the Church calendar focuses on Christ coming into the world as a baby born in Bethlehem over 2,000 years ago. From the fourth Sunday before Christmas until Christmas Eve, believers in Christ from all around the globe do two things: remember and anticipate.

REMEMBER

During Advent, we remember when our Savior stepped out of eternity into time to take on flesh. He came to live among us and offer His life for us, dying for our sins and rising from the grave. At Christmas, we don't just celebrate that He came; we celebrate why He came.

ANTICIPATE

We also anticipate Christ's promised return. After Jesus finished the work He had come to do, He promised He would return to establish His kingdom for all eternity. Celebrating Christmas is an act of worshiping the living Savior who will come again to make all things new.

Jesus Christ has come, and He is coming again. This is the heart of Advent. ❧

HOW TO STUDY WITH THE ONLINE COMMUNITY

For added community and conversation, join us in the **Joy to the World: Advent 2017** reading plan on the She Reads Truth app or on SheReadsTruth.com—where women from Flagstaff to Finland will be reading along with you!

Have a "He" in your life—a brother, father, husband, or friend? Invite him to join you by visiting HeReadsTruth.com or the He Reads Truth app, or by picking up the guy version of this book at ShopHeReadsTruth.com.

She Reads Truth is a community of women dedicated to reading the Word of God every day.
The Bible is living and active, breathed out by God, and we confidently hold it higher than anything
we can do or say. This book focuses primarily on Scripture with helpful and festive elements throughout.

SCRIPTURE READING

This study book includes daily Scripture readings to walk you through the Advent season.

JOURNALING SPACE

Each daily reading includes space for personal reflection and prayer.

GRACE DAY

Use this day to catch up on your reading, pray, and rest in the presence of the Lord. Consider trying one of the included recipes.

SUNDAYS IN ADVENT

This day marks the beginning of each week in Advent with a short prayer and Scripture passage.

Table of Contents

Pg

1   *The First Sunday of Advent* 17

2   The First Promise of the Messiah 18

3   God's Covenant with Abram 22

4   Christ's Birth Prophesied 26

     Prophecies of Jesus' Birth 30

5   The Stem of Jesse 32

6   The Glory of Little Bethlehem 36

7   *Grace Day* 42

8   *The Second Sunday of Advent* 45

     Merry Miscellany 46

9   The Law of God We Cannot Keep 48

10   Righteousness Through Christ 52

     God the Son 56

11   The Glory of the Lord 58

12   An All-Sufficient Sacrifice 62

13   All Nations Shall Find Peace 66

14   *Grace Day* 72

15   *The Third Sunday of Advent* 75

     Decking the Halls 76

16   The Birth of John the Baptist Foretold 78

17   Zechariah Struck Silent 82

18   The Angel Visits Mary and Joseph 86

     The Travels of Joseph, Mary, and Jesus   90

19   Mary Visits Elizabeth 92

20   The Birth of John the Baptist 96

21   *Grace Day* 102

CHRISTMAS WEEK

22   *The Fourth Sunday of Advent* 107

23   The Birth of Jesus 110

24   The Wise Men Visit the Christ Child 116

     Gold, Frankincense, and Myrrh 120

25   Jesus Presented in the Temple 122

     The Twelve Days of Christmas 126

26   Seek the Lord While He May Be Found . . . 128

27   Jesus Christ Is Lord 132

28   *Grace Day* 138

29   *The First Sunday After Christmas* 141

     For The Record 144

Recipes

Citrus Garland
Pg. 15

Butternut Squash
Soup pg. 40

Upside Down
Hot Chocolate

pg. 47

Rosemary and
Garlic Roast Beef &
Yorkshire Pudding
Popovers
pg. 100

Natalie's
Caramel Corn

pg. 136

Myers Family
Christmas Cookies
Pg. 70

Carols

This study includes the
*Repeat the Sounding Joy:
Songs for Advent* songbook.
Play through the familiar
Christmas hymns at the piano,
or use it to carol door-to-door
with friends and family.

20   JOY TO THE WORLD

38   AWAY IN A MANGER

68   THE FIRST NOEL

77   DECK THE HALLS

88   O COME, O COME, IMMANUEL

109   SILENT NIGHT! HOLY NIGHT!

114   ANGELS WE HAVE HEARD ON HIGH

BONUS CROSS STITCH PATTERN AND TUTORIAL pg. 142

When the She Reads Truth creative team began to imagine the 2017 Advent book back in July, we were given simple directions: **make it familiar and make it joyful**. This was just the inspiration we needed, and we quickly set about creating mood boards, styling sheet music, and building shot lists for the photoshoot that would provide the images you see in this book.

One of our first big decisions was awarding Salome the honor of being our hero typeface for not only the She Reads Truth Advent book, but for the He Reads Truth book and our Advent Scripture Calendar as well. You'll see it everywhere, and we hope that when you do, it strikes exactly the right nostalgic chord of familiar and joyful.

Of course, it wouldn't be a She Reads Truth Advent book without recipes and music. Food and song are important mediums of connection, whether among a handful of friends, across an online community, or through a family tradition shared across years and miles. We kept our mission in mind every step of the way as we selected carols and taste-tested caramel corn.

Perhaps our favorite creative detail of this book comes in the paper selection. From the opaque page at the beginning (it makes us think of the sheet of fancy paper covering a box of chocolates) to the green linen cover (we almost went red, but couldn't get over that pine-y green), creatively designing with paper gave us the opportunity to "gift wrap" this book like something from a boutique paper store. We sealed it with a white and gold foil ornament and bow by one of our favorite hand letterers, Eva Winters.

We're pleased and proud of the way our team created this book to be familiar and joyful. But God's words contained within its pages are the reason we celebrate. If, as you read them, you feel a certain amount of familiarity and joy, we will have done our job well—lending the already beautiful gospel the aesthetic beauty it deserves.

Joy to the world!

The She Reads Truth Creative Team

Citrus Garland

BY THE SHE READS TRUTH TEAM

MAKES: 10 FEET

This is a perfect use-what-you-have holiday activity. Using oranges will create a classic look, but you can go bigger with grapefruit, redder with blood oranges, or use lemons for a darker, caramelized color. We love any Christmastime project that takes minimal effort, treats multiple senses, and pays off for days and weeks after the work is done. Start these in the oven in the morning and your house will smell festive all day long!

INGREDIENTS

5-8 pieces of citrus (oranges, grapefruit, blood oranges, or lemons)

Whole cloves (optional)

DIRECTIONS

Preheat oven to 200°F.

Slice the citrus into 1/8"-1/4" slices and pat dry with a paper towel. Stick a few whole cloves into the oranges for added visual interest, or simply for added aroma while they cook.

Arrange on a cookie sheet lined with parchment paper and bake at 200°F for 5-6 hours, turning and checking every hour.

String up dried citrus on cotton string, jute cord, or ribbon. Drape your garland with greenery, across a window, or even vertically along a doorpost. Citrus will continue to dry as it hangs.

A Prayer for the First Sunday of Advent

Almighty God, give us grace to cast away the works of darkness, and put on the armor of light, now in the time of this mortal life in which your Son Jesus Christ came to visit us in great humility; that in the last day, when He shall come again in his glorious majesty to judge both the living and the dead, we may rise to the life immortal; through Him who lives and reigns with you and the Holy Spirit, one God, now and forever. Amen.

from *The Book of Common Prayer*

SCRIPTURE   Isaiah 9:6-7 ESV

⁶ For to us a child is born,
    to us a son is given;
and the government shall be upon his shoulder,
    and his name shall be called
Wonderful Counselor, Mighty God,
    Everlasting Father, Prince of Peace.
⁷ Of the increase of his government and of peace
    there will be no end,
on the throne of David and over his kingdom,
    to establish it and to uphold it
with justice and with righteousness
    from this time forth and forevermore.
The zeal of the LORD of hosts will do this.

DAY

2

The First Promise of the Messiah

Genesis 3:1-15

THE TEMPTATION AND THE FALL

¹ Now the serpent was the most cunning of all the wild animals that the Lord God had made. He said to the woman, "Did God really say, 'You can't eat from any tree in the garden'?"

² The woman said to the serpent, "We may eat the fruit from the trees in the garden. ³ But about the fruit of the tree in the middle of the garden, God said, 'You must not eat it or touch it, or you will die.'"

⁴ "No! You will not die," the serpent said to the woman. ⁵ "In fact, God knows that when you eat it your eyes will be opened and you will be like God, knowing good and evil." ⁶ The woman saw that the tree was good for food and delightful to look at, and that it was desirable for obtaining wisdom. So she took some of its fruit and ate it; she also gave some to her husband, who was with her, and he ate it. ⁷ Then the eyes of both of them were opened, and they knew they were naked; so they sewed fig leaves together and made coverings for themselves.

SIN'S CONSEQUENCES

⁸ Then the man and his wife heard the sound of the Lord God walking in the garden at the time of the evening breeze, and they hid from the Lord God among the trees of the garden. ⁹ So the Lord God called out to the man and said to him, "Where are you?"

¹⁰ And he said, "I heard you in the garden, and I was afraid because I was naked, so I hid."

¹¹ Then he asked, "Who told you that you were naked? Did you eat from the tree that I commanded you not to eat from?"

¹² The man replied, "The woman you gave to be with me—she gave me some fruit from the tree, and I ate."

¹³ So the Lord God asked the woman, "What is this you have done?"

And the woman said, "The serpent deceived me, and I ate."

continued

Joy to the World

text **ISAAC WATTS, 1719**
tune **LOWELL MASON, 1848**

The hymn "Joy to the World" is a jubilant proclamation of our Lord's birth. The verses are based on an English translation of Psalm 98 and were written and published in 1719 by English hymn writer Isaac Watts in his collection entitled *Psalms of David: Imitated in the Language of the New Testament.* It wasn't until 1839—one hundred twenty years later—that Lowell Mason, an American music teacher and composer, finally put Watts' words to melody, completing the song we sing today.

1 Joy to the world! the Lord is come: let earth re-ceive her King. Let ev-ery heart pre-pare Him room, and heaven and na-ture sing, and heaven and na-ture sing, and heaven, and heaven and na-ture sing.

2 Joy to the earth! the Sav-ior reigns; let men their songs em-ploy, while fields and floods, rocks, hills, and plains re-peat the sound-ing joy, re-peat the sound-ing joy, re-peat, re-peat the sound-ing joy.

3 No more let sin and sor-row grow nor thorns in-fest the ground; He comes to make His bless-ings flow far as the curse is found, far as the curse is found, far as, far as the curse is found.

4 He rules the world with truth and grace, and makes the na-tions prove the glo-ries of His right-eous-ness and won-ders of His love, and won-ders of His love, and won-ders, won-ders of His love.

¹⁴ So the Lord God said to the serpent:

Because you have done this,
you are cursed more than any livestock
and more than any wild animal.
You will move on your belly
and eat dust all the days of your life.
¹⁵ I will put hostility between you and the woman,
and between your offspring and her offspring.

He will strike your head, and you will strike his heel.

1 Corinthians 15:45-49

⁴⁵ So it is written, The first man Adam became a living being; the last Adam became a life-giving spirit. ⁴⁶ However, the spiritual is not first, but the natural, then the spiritual.

⁴⁷ The first man was from the earth, a man of dust; the second man is from heaven. ⁴⁸ Like the man of dust, so are those who are of the dust; like the man of heaven, so are those who are of heaven. ⁴⁹ And just as we have borne the image of the man of dust, we will also bear the image of the man of heaven.

Hebrews 2:14-16

¹⁴ Now since the children have flesh and blood in common, Jesus also shared in these, so that through his death he might destroy the one holding the power of death—that is, the devil— ¹⁵ and free those who were held in slavery all their lives by the fear of death. ¹⁶ For it is clear that he does not reach out to help angels, but to help Abraham's offspring.

DATE

NOTES

CHRISTMAS TRADITIONS

CHRISTMAS TREES

Whose idea was it to bring live trees indoors and decorate them with ornaments? The first Christmas trees, in the 1500s, were actually called "Paradise trees." They represented mankind's fall in the garden of Eden. Traditionally brought into the home on Christmas Eve, these trees were decorated with apples, symbolizing the fruit Adam and Eve ate from the tree of the knowledge of good and evil. Paper garlands, ribbons, nuts, round pastry wafers (symbolizing the communion wafer), and even candles were added to dress them up. Eventually, the apples were replaced with round bulb ornaments and the candles with the twinkle lights we're familiar with today.

God's Covenant with Abram

Genesis 12:1-9

THE CALL OF ABRAM

¹ The Lord said to Abram:

Go out from your land,
your relatives,
and your father's house
to the land that I will show you.
² I will make you into a great nation,
I will bless you,
I will make your name great,
and you will be a blessing.
³ I will bless those who bless you,
I will curse anyone who treats you with contempt,
and all the peoples on earth
will be blessed through you.

⁴ So Abram went, as the Lord had told him, and Lot went with him. Abram was seventy-five years old when he left Haran. ⁵ He took his wife Sarai, his nephew Lot, all the possessions they had accumulated, and the people they had acquired in Haran, and they set out for the land of Canaan. When they came to the land of Canaan, ⁶ Abram passed through the land to the site of Shechem, at the oak of Moreh. (At that time the Canaanites were in the land.) ⁷ The Lord appeared to Abram and said, "To your offspring I will give this land." So he built an altar there to the Lord who had appeared to him. ⁸ From there he moved on to the hill country east of Bethel and pitched his tent, with Bethel on the west and Ai on the east. He built an altar to the Lord there, and he called on the name of the Lord. ⁹ Then Abram journeyed by stages to the Negev.

Genesis 21:1-7

THE BIRTH OF ISAAC

¹ The Lord came to Sarah as he had said, and the Lord did for Sarah what he had promised. ² Sarah became pregnant and bore a son to Abraham in his old age, at the appointed time God had told him. ³ Abraham named his son who was born to him—the one Sarah bore to him—Isaac. ⁴ When his son Isaac was eight days old, Abraham circumcised him, as God had commanded him. ⁵ Abraham was a hundred years old when his son Isaac was born to him.

[6] Sarah said, "God has made me laugh, and everyone who hears will laugh with me." [7] She also said, "Who would have told Abraham that Sarah would nurse children? Yet I have borne a son for him in his old age."

Genesis 22:15-18

[15] Then the angel of the LORD called to Abraham a second time from heaven [16] and said, "By myself I have sworn," this is the LORD's declaration: "Because you have done this thing and have not withheld your only son, [17] I will indeed bless you and make your offspring as numerous as the stars of the sky and the sand on the seashore. Your offspring will possess the city gates of their enemies. [18] And all the nations of the earth will be blessed by your offspring because you have obeyed my command."

John 8:56-58

[56] "Your father Abraham rejoiced to see my day; he saw it and was glad."

[57] The Jews replied, "You aren't fifty years old yet, and you've seen Abraham?"

[58] Jesus said to them,

"Truly I tell you, before Abraham was, I am."

DATE   NOTES

DAY

4

Christ's Birth Prophesied

Isaiah 7:10-14

THE IMMANUEL PROPHECY

10 Then the LORD spoke again to Ahaz: 11 "Ask for a sign from the LORD your God—it can be as deep as Sheol or as high as heaven."

12 But Ahaz replied, "I will not ask. I will not test the LORD."

13 Isaiah said, "Listen, house of David! Is it not enough for you to try the patience of men? Will you also try the patience of my God? 14 Therefore,

the Lord himself will give you a sign: See, the virgin will conceive, have a son, and name him Immanuel."

Jeremiah 23:1-8

THE LORD AND HIS SHEEP

1 "Woe to the shepherds who destroy and scatter the sheep of my pasture!" This is the LORD's declaration. 2 "Therefore, this is what the LORD, the God of Israel, says about the shepherds who tend my people: You have scattered my flock, banished them, and have not attended to them. I am

about to attend to you because of your evil acts"—this is the LORD's declaration. ³ "I will gather the remnant of my flock from all the lands where I have banished them, and I will return them to their grazing land. They will become fruitful and numerous. ⁴ I will raise up shepherds over them who will tend them. They will no longer be afraid or discouraged, nor will any be missing." This is the LORD's declaration.

THE RIGHTEOUS BRANCH OF DAVID

⁵ "Look, the days are coming"—this is the LORD's declaration—

"when I will raise up a Righteous Branch for David.
He will reign wisely as king
and administer justice and righteousness in the land.
⁶ In his days Judah will be saved,
and Israel will dwell securely.
This is the name he will be called:
The LORD Is Our Righteousness.

⁷ "Look, the days are coming"—the LORD's declaration—"when it will no longer be said, 'As the LORD lives who brought the Israelites from the land of Egypt,' ⁸ but, 'As the LORD lives, who brought and led the descendants of the house of Israel from the land of the north and from all the other countries where I had banished them.' They will dwell once more in their own land."

Matthew 1:22-23

²² Now all this took place to fulfill what was spoken by the Lord through the prophet:

²³ See, the virgin will become pregnant
and give birth to a son,
and they will name him Immanuel,

which is translated "God is with us."

1 John 4:7-10

KNOWING GOD THROUGH LOVE

⁷ Dear friends, let us love one another, because love is from God, and everyone who loves has been born of God and knows God. ⁸ The one who does not love does not know God, because God is love. ⁹ God's love was revealed among us in this way:

God sent his one and only Son into the world so that we might live through him.

¹⁰ Love consists in this: not that we loved God, but that he loved us and sent his Son to be the atoning sacrifice for our sins.

Revelation 21:3-5

³ Then I heard a loud voice from the throne: Look, God's dwelling is with humanity, and he will live with them. They will be his peoples, and God himself will be with them and will be their God. ⁴ He will wipe away every tear from their eyes. Death will be no more; grief, crying, and pain will be no more, because the previous things have passed away.

⁵ Then the one seated on the throne said, "Look, I am making everything new." He also said, "Write, because these words are faithful and true."

DATE

NOTES

Prophecies of Jesus' Birth

The Old Testament is filled with prophecy about the Messiah's coming. Many of those prophecies centered specifically on His birth. Here are some of the prophecies which point to Jesus as the promised Savior and Lord.

THE SAVIOR WILL BE

the Son of Man	the Son of God	born of a virgin	called "Lord"	called "Immanuel"	a blessing to the world from the line of Abraham	the Star of Jacob
OLD TESTAMENT PROPHECY						
GENESIS 3:15 I will put hostility between you and the woman, and between your offspring and her offspring. He will strike your head, and you will strike his heel.	PSALM 2:7 I will declare the LORD'S decree. He said to me, "You are my Son; today I have become your Father."	ISAIAH 7:14 Therefore, the Lord himself will give you a sign: See, the virgin will conceive, have a son…	JEREMIAH 23:6 In his days Judah will be saved, and Israel will dwell securely. This is the name he will be called: The LORD Is Our Righteousness.	ISAIAH 7:14 See, the virgin will conceive, have a son, and name him Immanuel.	GENESIS 22:18 And all the nations of the earth will be blessed by your offspring because you have obeyed my command.	NUMBERS 24:17 I see him, but not now; I perceive him, but not near. A star will come from Jacob, and a scepter will arise from Israel.
FULFILLED IN CHRIST						
GALATIANS 4:4 When the time came to completion, God sent his Son, born of a woman, born under the law…	LUKE 3:22 …and the Holy Spirit descended on him in a physical appearance like a dove. And a voice came from heaven: "You are my beloved Son; with you I am well-pleased."	LUKE 1:26-27 In the sixth month, the angel Gabriel was sent by God to a town in Galilee called Nazareth, to a virgin engaged to a man named Joseph, of the house of David. The virgin's name was Mary.	LUKE 2:11 Today in the city of David a Savior was born for you, who is the Messiah, the Lord.	MATTHEW 1:22-23 Now all this took place to fulfill what was spoken by the Lord through the prophet: See, the virgin… will name him Immanuel, which is translated "God is with us."	MATTHEW 1:1-2 An account of the genealogy of Jesus Christ, the Son of David, the Son of Abraham: Abraham fathered Isaac…	LUKE 1:33 He will reign over the house of Jacob forever, and his kingdom will have no end.

on King David's throne forever	born in Bethlehem	one to whom shepherds would bow	one to whom kings would bow	called out of Egypt	born into sorrow
2 SAMUEL 7:12-13 When your time comes and you rest with your fathers, I will raise up after you your descendant, who will come from your body, and I will establish his kingdom. He is the one who will build a house for my name, and I will establish the throne of his kingdom forever.	MICAH 5:2 Bethlehem Ephrathah, you are small among the clans of Judah; one will come from you to be ruler over Israel for me. His origin is from antiquity, from ancient times.	PSALM 72:9 May desert tribes kneel before him…	PSALM 72:10-11 May the kings of Tarshish and the coasts and islands bring tribute, the kings of Sheba and Seba offer gifts. Let all kings bow in homage to him, all nations serve him.	HOSEA 11:1 When Israel was a child, I loved him, and out of Egypt I called my son.	JEREMIAH 31:15 This is what the LORD says: A voice was heard in Ramah, a lament with bitter weeping—Rachel weeping for her children, refusing to be comforted for her children because they are no more.
LUKE 1:32 He will be great and will be called the Son of the Most High, and the Lord God will give him the throne of his father David.	MATTHEW 2:3-5 When King Herod heard this, he was deeply disturbed, and all Jerusalem with him. So he assembled all the chief priests and scribes of the people and asked them where the Christ would be born. "In Bethlehem of Judea," they told him, "because this is what was written by the prophet…"	LUKE 2:20 The shepherds returned, glorifying and praising God for all the things they had seen and heard, which were just as they had been told.	MATTHEW 2:11 Entering the house, they saw the child with Mary his mother, and falling to their knees, they worshiped him. Then they opened their treasures and presented him with gifts: gold, frankincense, and myrrh.	MATTHEW 2:14-15 So he got up, took the child and his mother during the night, and escaped to Egypt. He stayed there until Herod's death, so that what was spoken by the Lord through the prophet might be fulfilled: Out of Egypt I called my Son.	MATTHEW 2:16-17 Then Herod, when he realized that he had been outwitted by the wise men, flew into a rage. He gave orders to massacre all the boys in and around Bethlehem who were two years old and under, in keeping with the time he had learned from the wise men. Then what was spoken through Jeremiah the prophet was fulfilled…

DAY

5

The Stem of Jesse

1 Samuel 16:6-13

⁶ When they arrived, Samuel saw Eliab and said, "Certainly the LORD's anointed one is here before him."

⁷ But the LORD said to Samuel, "Do not look at his appearance or his stature because I have rejected him. Humans do not see what the LORD sees, for humans see what is visible, but the LORD sees the heart."

⁸ Jesse called Abinadab and presented him to Samuel. "The LORD hasn't chosen this one either," Samuel said. ⁹ Then Jesse presented Shammah, but Samuel said, "The Lord hasn't chosen this one either." ¹⁰ After Jesse presented seven of his sons to him, Samuel told Jesse, "The LORD hasn't chosen any of these." ¹¹ Samuel asked him, "Are these all the sons you have?"

"There is still the youngest," he answered, "but right now he's tending the sheep." Samuel told Jesse, "Send for him. We won't sit down to eat until he gets here." ¹² So Jesse sent for him. He had beautiful eyes and a healthy, handsome appearance.

Then the LORD said, "Anoint him, for he is the one." ¹³ So Samuel took the horn of oil and anointed him in the presence of his brothers, and the Spirit of the LORD came powerfully on David from that day forward. Then Samuel set out and went to Ramah.

Isaiah 11:1-6

REIGN OF THE DAVIDIC KING

¹ Then a shoot will grow from the stump of Jesse,
and a branch from his roots will bear fruit.
² The Spirit of the LORD will rest on him—
a Spirit of wisdom and understanding,
a Spirit of counsel and strength,
a Spirit of knowledge and of the fear of the LORD.
³ His delight will be in the fear of the LORD.
He will not judge
by what he sees with his eyes,
he will not execute justice
by what he hears with his ears,
⁴ but he will judge the poor righteously
and execute justice for the oppressed of the land.

He will strike the land
with a scepter from his mouth,
and he will kill the wicked
with a command from his lips.
⁵ Righteousness will be a belt around his hips;
faithfulness will be a belt around his waist.

⁶ The wolf will dwell with the lamb,
and the leopard will lie down with the goat.
The calf, the young lion, and the fattened calf will
be together,
and a child will lead them.

Isaiah 53:2-3

² He grew up before him like a young plant
and like a root out of dry ground.
He didn't have an impressive form
or majesty that we should look at him,
no appearance that we should desire him.
³ He was despised and rejected by men,
a man of suffering who knew what sickness was.
He was like someone people turned away from;
he was despised, and we didn't value him.

Matthew 12:22-23

²² Then a demon-possessed man who was blind and unable
to speak was brought to him. He healed him, so that the man
could both speak and see. ²³ All the crowds were astounded
and said, "Could this be the Son of David?"

Matthew 22:41-46

THE QUESTION ABOUT THE CHRIST

⁴¹ While the Pharisees were together, Jesus questioned them,
⁴² "What do you think about the Messiah? Whose son is he?"

They replied, "David's."

⁴³ He asked them, "How is it then that David, inspired by
the Spirit, calls him 'Lord':

⁴⁴ The Lord declared to my Lord,
'Sit at my right hand
until I put your enemies under your feet'?

⁴⁵ "If David calls him 'Lord,' how then can he be his son?"
⁴⁶ No one was able to answer him at all, and from that day no
one dared to question him anymore.

Revelation 22:16

"I, Jesus, have sent
my angel to attest these
things to you for the
churches. I am the root
and descendant of David,
the bright morning star."

DATE

NOTES

DAY

6

The Glory of Little Bethlehem

Micah 5:2-6

² Bethlehem Ephrathah,
you are small among the clans of Judah;
one will come from you
to be ruler over Israel for me.
His origin is from antiquity,
from ancient times.
³ Therefore, Israel will be abandoned until the time
when she who is in labor has given birth;
then the rest of the ruler's brothers will return
to the people of Israel.
⁴ He will stand and shepherd them
in the strength of the LORD,
in the majestic name of the LORD his God.
They will live securely,
for then his greatness will extend
to the ends of the earth.

⁵ He will be their peace.

When Assyria invades our land,
when it marches against our fortresses,
we will raise against it seven shepherds,
even eight leaders of men.
⁶ They will shepherd the land of Assyria with the sword,
the land of Nimrod with a drawn blade.
So he will rescue us from Assyria
when it invades our land,
when it marches against our territory.

Numbers 24:17-18

¹⁷ I see him, but not now;
I perceive him, but not near.
A star will come from Jacob,
and a scepter will arise from Israel.
He will smash the forehead of Moab
and strike down all the Shethites.
¹⁸ Edom will become a possession;
Seir will become a possession of its enemies,
but Israel will be triumphant.

Luke 2:4

Joseph also went up from the town of Nazareth in Galilee, to Judea, to the city of David, which is called Bethlehem, because he was of the house and family line of David.

John 7:40-44

THE PEOPLE ARE DIVIDED OVER JESUS

⁴⁰ When some from the crowd heard these words, they said, "This truly is the Prophet." ⁴¹ Others said, "This is the Messiah." But some said, "Surely the Messiah doesn't come from Galilee, does he? ⁴² Doesn't the Scripture say that the Messiah comes from David's offspring and from the town of Bethlehem, where David lived?" ⁴³ So the crowd was divided because of him. ⁴⁴ Some of them wanted to seize him, but no one laid hands on him.

continued

Away in a Manger

text AMERICAN, 1885
tune WILIAM J. KIRKPATRICK, 1895

This beloved hymn is often an integral part of teaching children the basic story of Jesus' birth. It is regularly attributed to German theological reformer Martin Luther as "Luther's Cradle Hymn," supposedly a lullaby for his own children. But the lyrics actually may have been lifted from a children's Sunday school book published in Philadelphia, Pennsylvania, in 1885. Regardless, in 1887, writer James R. Murray published the lyrics as Luther's in a collection entitled *Dainty Songs for Lads and Lasses.*

1. A - way in a man - ger, no crib for a bed, the lit - tle Lord
2. The cat - tle are low - ing, the ba - by a - wakes, but lit - tle Lord
3. Be near me, Lord Je - sus, I ask Thee to stay close by me for -

Je - sus lay down His sweet head; the stars in the bright sky look
Je - sus no cry - ing He makes; I love Thee, Lord Je - sus! Look
ev - er, and love me, I pray; bless all the dear child - ren in

down where He lay, the lit - tle Lord Je - sus, a - sleep on the hay.
down from the sky, and stay by my cra - dle till morn - ing is nigh.
Thy ten - der care, and fit us for heav - en to live with Thee there.

John 10:11-18

¹¹ "I am the good shepherd. The good shepherd lays down his life for the sheep. ¹² The hired hand, since he is not the shepherd and doesn't own the sheep, leaves them and runs away when he sees a wolf coming. The wolf then snatches and scatters them. ¹³ This happens because he is a hired hand and doesn't care about the sheep.

¹⁴ "I am the good shepherd. I know my own, and my own know me, ¹⁵ just as the Father knows me, and I know the Father. I lay down my life for the sheep. ¹⁶ But I have other sheep that are not from this sheep pen; I must bring them also, and they will listen to my voice.

Then there will be one flock, one shepherd.

¹⁷ This is why the Father loves me, because I lay down my life so that I may take it up again. ¹⁸ No one takes it from me, but I lay it down on my own. I have the right to lay it down, and I have the right to take it up again. I have received this command from my Father."

Butternut Squash Soup

BY AMANDA BARNHART
SERVES: 4

A bowl of creamy soup in the dead of winter is one of the things I look forward to most during the holidays. This recipe can be made weeks in advance and frozen—perfect to serve when family visits or as an entree substitute for vegetarians. The comforting texture and delicious, subtle flavors are sure to make even the toughest vegetable skeptic a fan.

INGREDIENTS

1 tablespoon olive oil

2 small shallots, chopped

2 cloves garlic, minced

1 medium butternut squash, skin & seeds removed, cubed (roughly 6 cups)

Salt & pepper

1/2 tablespoon paprika

1/4 teaspoon ground cinnamon

2 cups vegetable stock

1 14-ounce can unsweetened coconut milk

1 tablespoon honey

1 8-ounce can butter beans, rinsed & drained (optional, for added protein)

1-2 rosemary sprigs, removed from stem & finely chopped (for garnish)

DIRECTIONS

Heat olive oil in a Dutch oven or large pot and add diced shallots and garlic over medium heat. Sauté 2 minutes, until soft.

Add cubed butternut squash, paprika, cinnamon, and salt and pepper to taste. Cover and let cook 5 minutes, stirring occasionally, at medium-low heat. Add more olive oil as needed to keep ingredients from sticking to pot.

Add vegetable stock, coconut milk, honey, and butter beans. Bring to a boil. Reduce heat to low, then cover and let simmer 15 minutes, or until butternut squash is soft.

Using a food processor, blender, or hand mixer, purée soup until it is silky smooth.

Pour the purée back into pot and add more seasoning to taste.

Garnish each bowl with rosemary and fresh cracked pepper. Serve with a side of crusty bread and a drizzle of coconut milk.

DAY

7

DATE

Grace Day

Advent is a season of anticipation and celebration. We long for the promised Savior's return, even as we rejoice that He has already come to us. Use this day to pause and reflect on this verse which celebrates the gift of salvation through Jesus, God's Son.

God's love was revealed among us in this way: God sent his one and only Son into the world so that we might live through him.

I JOHN 4:9

A Prayer for the Second Sunday of Advent

Merciful God, who sent your messengers the prophets to preach repentance and prepare the way for our salvation: Give us grace to heed their warnings and forsake our sins, that we may greet with joy the coming of Jesus Christ our Redeemer; who lives and reigns with you and the Holy Spirit, one God, now and forever. Amen.

from *The Book of Common Prayer*

SCRIPTURE   Joel 2:12-13

[12] Even now—
this is the LORD's declaration—
turn to me with all your heart,
with fasting, weeping, and mourning.
[13] Tear your hearts,
not just your clothes,
and return to the LORD your God.
For he is gracious and compassionate,
slow to anger, abounding in faithful love,
and he relents from sending disaster.

Each year, Americans mail more than 3 billion **Christmas cards.** Many of these letters bear the year's official Christmas stamp, which the United States Postal Service began issuing annually in 1962.

"Jingle Bells"

was originally written as a Thanksgiving song. Composer James Pierpont wrote the song in 1857 for his Sunday School class, titling it "One Horse Open Sleigh." A century later, "Jingle Bells" became the first song broadcast from space when Gemini 6 astronauts, Tom Stafford and Wally Schirra, sang it over the radio on December 16, 1965.

The United States didn't declare Christmas an official federal holiday until

1870.

On the state level, Alabama was the first to recognize Christmas as a holiday in 1836, and Oklahoma was the last, in 1907.

17%

of all annual retail sales in the United States are comprised of Christmas gifts and purchases. Bestselling toys over the last century include Mr. Potato Head, Tinker Toys, Yo-Yos, Slinkys, BB guns, Hula Hoops, Barbies, Rubik's Cubes, and LEGO sets. In fact, a recent study reported that nearly 28 LEGO sets are sold every second during the holidays.

In 2008, residents of Bethel, Maine, built the world's tallest snow woman, named Olympia, which stood a whopping

122 feet tall.

It took 170 people two months to build her, and she weighed over 13 million pounds. It took until the end of July for her to melt completely.

Irving Berlin's "White Christmas" is estimated to be the bestselling single in history, with over

100 MILLION

sales worldwide.

"Silent Night" is the most recorded Christmas song in history, with nearly 750 different versions copyrighted since 1978. If you listened to each version, back-to-back, it would take over

37 hours.

BE CAREFUL!

From hanging lights on the eaves to taking the turkey out of the oven, celebrating Christmas can be dangerous. The Consumer Product Safety Commission estimates that around 15,000 Americans make **unplanned emergency room visits** each holiday season because of decorating and cooking related accidents.

On Christmas Day of 1914, during World War I, German and British soldiers declared a temporary truce and celebrated the day together in the field between their battle lines known as **"No Man's Land."** They decorated their shelters, exchanged gifts, and played games before resuming fighting the following day.

Photo by Alyssa Valletta

Warm drinks and crisp air are staples of the season. This year, our team put a twist on traditional hot cocoa by turning it upside down with white hot chocolate and chocolate whip. Try the chocolate whipped cream on other sweet treats this season, too—like cakes, cupcakes, or pies. We think you'll love it!

Upside Down Hot Chocolate

BY THE SHE READS TRUTH TEAM

SERVES: 4

WHITE HOT CHOCOLATE
INGREDIENTS

4 cups whole milk

1 cup good quality white chocolate chips or chopped white chocolate

1 teaspoon pure vanilla extract

Pinch of salt

DIRECTIONS

Combine milk, white chocolate, vanilla, and salt in a medium saucepan over medium-low heat.

Whisk continuously until the chocolate has melted and the mixture is smooth. (Do not boil.) Serve immediately with chocolate whipped cream.

CHOCOLATE WHIPPED CREAM
INGREDIENTS

2 cups heavy cream

1/4 cup cocoa powder

1/2 cup powdered sugar

White chocolate chips, chocolate shavings, marshmallows, candy canes (optional, for garnish)

DIRECTIONS

Place a metal mixing bowl and whisk attachment in the freezer for 15 minutes.

Remove bowl and whisk from freezer. Combine heavy cream, cocoa powder, and powdered sugar in bowl. Beat with an electric mixer for 3-5 minutes, or until it holds its shape.

Scoop a dollop of whip onto hot chocolate.

Garnish with white chocolate chips, chocolate shavings, marshmallows, candy canes, or cinnamon sticks.

Leftovers can be refrigerated up to 3 days.

DAY

9

The Law of God
We Cannot Keep

Exodus 20:1-17

THE TEN COMMANDMENTS

¹ Then God spoke all these words:

² I am the LORD your God, who brought you out of the land of Egypt, out of the place of slavery.

³ Do not have other gods besides me.

⁴ Do not make an idol for yourself, whether in the shape of anything in the heavens above or on the earth below or in the waters under the earth. ⁵ Do not bow in worship to them, and do not serve them; for I, the LORD your God, am a jealous God, punishing the children for the fathers' iniquity, to the third and fourth generations of those who hate me, ⁶ but showing faithful love to a thousand generations of those who love me and keep my commands.

⁷ Do not misuse the name of the LORD your God, because the LORD will not leave anyone unpunished who misuses his name.

⁸ Remember the Sabbath day, to keep it holy: ⁹ You are to labor six days and do all your work, ¹⁰ but the seventh day is a Sabbath to the LORD your God. You must not do any work—you, your son or daughter, your male or female servant, your livestock, or the resident alien who is within your city gates. ¹¹ For the LORD made the heavens and the earth, the sea, and everything in them in six days; then he rested on the seventh day. Therefore the LORD blessed the Sabbath day and declared it holy.

¹² Honor your father and your mother so that you may have a long life in the land that the LORD your God is giving you.

¹³ Do not murder.

¹⁴ Do not commit adultery.

¹⁵ Do not steal.

¹⁶ Do not give false testimony against your neighbor.

¹⁷ Do not covet your neighbor's house. Do not covet your neighbor's wife, his male or female servant, his ox or donkey, or anything that belongs to your neighbor.

Matthew 5:17-19

CHRIST FULFILLS THE LAW

[17] "Don't think that I came to abolish the Law or the Prophets. I did not come to abolish but to fulfill. [18] For truly I tell you, until heaven and earth pass away, not the smallest letter or one stroke of a letter will pass away from the law until all things are accomplished. [19] Therefore, whoever breaks one of the least of these commands and teaches others to do the same will be called least in the kingdom of heaven. But whoever does and teaches these commands will be called great in the kingdom of heaven."

Romans 8:1-4

THE LIFE-GIVING SPIRIT

[1] Therefore, there is now no condemnation for those in Christ Jesus, [2] because the law of the Spirit of life in Christ Jesus has set you free from the law of sin and death.

[3] What the law could not do since it was weakened by the flesh, God did.

He condemned sin in the flesh by sending his own Son in the likeness of sinful flesh as a sin offering, [4] in order that the law's requirement would be fulfilled in us who do not walk according to the flesh but according to the Spirit.

DATE

NOTES

DAY

10

CHRISTMAS TRADITIONS

CHRISTMAS GIFTS

Why do we exchange gifts during Christmas?
At the heart of the Christmas holiday is the birthday celebration of Jesus, our Savior. The exchanging of wrapped gifts at Christmastime dates back as early as the fifth century, and is linked to the gifts the magi gave to Jesus—gold, frankincense, and myrrh. Scripture tells us "it is more blessed to give than to receive" (Ac 20:35), and that when we give to those around us, we are giving to Jesus as well (Mt 25:40).

52

Righteousness Through Christ

Romans 3:21-28

THE RIGHTEOUSNESS OF GOD THROUGH FAITH

[21] But now, apart from the law, the righteousness of God has been revealed, attested by the Law and the Prophets. [22] The righteousness of God is through faith in Jesus Christ to all who believe, since there is no distinction. [23] For all have sinned and fall short of the glory of God. [24] They are justified freely by his grace through the redemption that is in Christ Jesus. [25] God presented him as an atoning sacrifice in his blood, received through faith, to demonstrate his righteousness, because in his restraint God passed over the sins previously committed. [26] God presented him to demonstrate his righteousness at the present time, so that he would be righteous and declare righteous the one who has faith in Jesus.

BOASTING EXCLUDED

[27] Where, then, is boasting? It is excluded. By what kind of law? By one of works? No, on the contrary, by a law of faith. [28] For we conclude that a person is justified by faith apart from the works of the law.

John 1:1-5

PROLOGUE

[1] In the beginning was the Word, and the Word was with God, and the Word was God. [2] He was with God in the beginning. [3] All things were created through him, and apart from him not one thing was created that has been created. [4] In him was life, and that life was the light of men. [5] That light shines in the darkness, and yet the darkness did not overcome it.

John 1:14-18

[14] The Word became flesh and dwelt among us. We observed his glory, the glory as the one and only Son from the Father, full of grace and truth. [15] (John testified concerning him and exclaimed, "This was the one of whom I said, 'The one coming after me ranks ahead of me, because he existed before me.'") [16] Indeed, we have all received grace upon grace from his fullness, [17] for the law was given through Moses; grace and truth came through Jesus Christ.

[18] No one has ever seen God. The one and only Son, who is himself God and is at the Father's side—he has revealed him.

Ephesians 1:7-10

[7] In him we have redemption through his blood, the forgiveness of our trespasses, according to the riches of his grace [8] that he richly poured out on us with all wisdom and understanding. [9] He made known to us the mystery of his will, according to his good pleasure that he purposed in Christ [10] as a plan for the right time—to bring everything together in Christ, both things in heaven and things on earth in him.

Colossians 1:13-14

[13] He has rescued us from the domain of darkness and transferred us into the kingdom of the Son he loves. [14] In him we have redemption, the forgiveness of sins.

DATE

NOTES

GOD
THE
SON

An Excerpt from The Book of Common Prayer Catechism

A catechism is a series of questions and answers used to teach foundational doctrines of the faith.

What do we mean when we say that Jesus is the only Son of God?

We mean that Jesus is the only perfect image of the Father, and shows us the nature of God.

MT 3:16-17, JN 1:14-18, COL 1:15-17, COL 2:9, HEB 1:2-3, IJN 5:1-13

What is the nature of God revealed in Jesus?

God is love.

JN 3:16, RM 5:8, RM 8:38-39, 2TH 3:5, IJN 4:7-16

What do we mean when we say that Jesus was conceived by the power of the Holy Spirit and became incarnate from the Virgin Mary?

We mean that by God's own act, His divine Son received our human nature from the Virgin Mary, His mother.

MT 1:23, LK 1:26-38, LK 2:6-7, GL 4:4-5, PHP 2:6-7

Why did He take our human nature?

The divine Son became human, so that in Him human beings might be adopted as children of God, and be made heirs of God's kingdom.

MT 20:28, JN 1:10-13, JN 3:16-17, RM 8:13-17, GL 3:26-29, HEB 2:17

What is the great importance of Jesus' suffering and death?

By His obedience, even to suffering and death, Jesus made the offering which we could not make; in Him we are freed from the power of sin and reconciled to God.

IS 53:5-6, 10-12, MK 10:45, RM 3:23-25, IJN 2:2, IPT 2:24

What is the significance of Jesus' resurrection?

By His resurrection, Jesus overcame death and opened for us the way of eternal life.

IS 25:8, RM 1:3-4, ICO 15:24-26, 2CO 5:14-15, EPH 2:1-7, COL 1:21-22, 2TM 1:10

What do we mean when we say that He ascended into heaven and is seated at the right hand of the Father?

We mean that Jesus took our human nature into heaven where He now reigns with the Father and intercedes for us.

AC 1:9-11, AC 7:55-56, RM 8:10-11, RM 8:34, ICO 15:20-22, COL 3:1, HEB 8:1-6

How can we share in His victory over sin, suffering, and death?

We share in His victory when we are baptized into the new covenant and become living members of Christ.

RM 6:1-3, RM 8:37, 2CO 5:17, GL 2:20, EPH 6:10-18, TI 3:5

DAY

11

The Glory of the Lord

Isaiah 9:2-5

[2] The people walking in darkness
have seen a great light;
a light has dawned
on those living in the land of darkness.
[3] You have enlarged the nation
and increased its joy.
The people have rejoiced before you
as they rejoice at harvest time
and as they rejoice when dividing spoils.
[4] For you have shattered their oppressive yoke
and the rod on their shoulders,
the staff of their oppressor,
just as you did on the day of Midian.
[5] For every trampling boot of battle
and the bloodied garments of war
will be burned as fuel for the fire.

Isaiah 60:1-5

[1] Arise, shine, for your light has come,
and the glory of the LORD shines over you.
[2] For look, darkness will cover the earth,

and total darkness the peoples;
but the LORD will shine over you,
and his glory will appear over you.
[3] Nations will come to your light,
and kings to your shining brightness.
[4] Raise your eyes and look around:
they all gather and come to you;
your sons will come from far away,
and your daughters on the hips of nannies.
[5] Then you will see and be radiant,
and your heart will tremble and rejoice,
because the riches of the sea will become yours
and the wealth of the nations will come to you.

Matthew 4:12-17

MINISTRY IN GALILEE

[12] When he heard that John had been arrested, he withdrew into Galilee. [13] He left Nazareth and went to live in Capernaum by the sea, in the region of Zebulun and Naphtali. [14] This was to fulfill what was spoken through the prophet Isaiah:

¹⁵ Land of Zebulun and land of Naphtali,
along the road by the sea, beyond the Jordan,
Galilee of the Gentiles.
¹⁶ The people who live in darkness
have seen a great light,
and for those living in the land of the shadow of death,
a light has dawned.

¹⁷ From then on Jesus began to preach, "Repent, because the kingdom of heaven has come near."

John 8:12

Jesus spoke to them again:

"I am the light of the world. Anyone who follows me will never walk in the darkness but will have the light of life."

2 Corinthians 8:9

For you know the grace of our Lord Jesus Christ: Though he was rich, for your sake he became poor, so that by his poverty you might become rich.

Revelation 22:1-5

¹ Then he showed me the river of the water of life, clear as crystal, flowing from the throne of God and of the Lamb ² down the middle of the city's main street. The tree of life was on each side of the river, bearing twelve kinds of fruit, producing its fruit every month. The leaves of the tree are for healing the nations, ³ and there will no longer be any curse. The throne of God and of the Lamb will be in the city, and his servants will worship him. ⁴ They will see his face, and his name will be on their foreheads. ⁵ Night will be no more; people will not need the light of a lamp or the light of the sun, because the Lord God will give them light, and they will reign forever and ever.

DATE

NOTES

DAY

12

An All-Sufiicient Sacrifice

Isaiah 1:11, 18

11 "What are all your sacrifices to me?"
asks the LORD.
"I have had enough of burnt offerings and rams
and the fat of well-fed cattle;
I have no desire for the blood of bulls,
lambs, or male goats.

18 "Come, let us settle this,"
says the LORD.
"Though your sins are scarlet,
they will be as white as snow;
though they are crimson red,
they will be like wool."

Isaiah 53:4-5

4 Yet he himself bore our sicknesses,
and he carried our pains;
but we in turn regarded him stricken,
struck down by God, and afflicted.
5 But he was pierced because of our rebellion,
crushed because of our iniquities;
punishment for our peace was on him,
and we are healed by his wounds.

John 1:29

The next day John saw Jesus coming toward him and said,

"Here is the Lamb of God, who takes away the sin of the world!"

Hebrews 9:11-14

NEW COVENANT MINISTRY

11 But Christ has appeared as a high priest of the good things that have come. In the greater and more perfect tabernacle not made with hands (that is, not of this creation), 12 he entered the most holy place once for all time, not by the blood of goats and calves, but by his own blood, having obtained eternal redemption. 13 For if the blood of goats and bulls and the ashes of a young cow, sprinkling those who are defiled, sanctify for the purification of the flesh, 14 how much more will the blood of Christ, who through the eternal Spirit offered himself without blemish to God, cleanse our consciences from dead works so that we can serve the living God?

Hebrews 10:1-14

THE PERFECT SACRIFICE

[1] Since the law has only a shadow of the good things to come, and not the reality itself of those things, it can never perfect the worshipers by the same sacrifices they continually offer year after year. [2] Otherwise, wouldn't they have stopped being offered, since the worshipers, purified once and for all, would no longer have any consciousness of sins? [3] But in the sacrifices there is a reminder of sins year after year. [4] For it is impossible for the blood of bulls and goats to take away sins.

[5] Therefore, as he was coming into the world, he said:

> You did not desire sacrifice and offering,
> but you prepared a body for me.
> [6] You did not delight
> in whole burnt offerings and sin offerings.
> [7] Then I said, "See—
> it is written about me
> in the scroll—
> I have come to do your will, O God."

[8] After he says above, You did not desire or delight in sacrifices and offerings, whole burnt offerings and sin offerings (which are offered according to the law), [9] he then says, See, I have come to do your will. He takes away the first to establish the second. [10] By this will, we have been sanctified through the offering of the body of Jesus Christ once for all time.

[11] Every priest stands day after day ministering and offering the same sacrifices time after time, which can never take away sins. [12] But this man,

after offering one sacrifice for sins forever,

sat down at the right hand of God. [13] He is now waiting until his enemies are made his footstool. [14] For by one offering he has perfected forever those who are sanctified.

DATE

NOTES

DAY

13

All Nations Shall Find Peace

Micah 4:1-7

THE LORD'S RULE FROM RESTORED ZION

¹ In the last days
the mountain of the LORD's house
will be established
at the top of the mountains
and will be raised above the hills.
Peoples will stream to it,
² and many nations will come and say,
"Come, let us go up to the mountain of the LORD,
to the house of the God of Jacob.
He will teach us about his ways
so we may walk in his paths."
For instruction will go out of Zion
and the word of the Lord from Jerusalem.
³ He will settle disputes among many peoples
and provide arbitration for strong nations
that are far away.
They will beat their swords into plows
and their spears into pruning knives.
Nation will not take up the sword against nation,
and they will never again train for war.
⁴ But each person will sit under his grapevine
and under his fig tree
with no one to frighten him.
For the mouth of the Lord of Armies
has spoken.
⁵ Though all the peoples each walk
in the name of their gods,
we will walk in the name of the LORD our God
forever and ever.

⁶ On that day—
    this is the LORD's declaration—
I will assemble the lame
and gather the scattered,
those I have injured.
⁷ I will make the lame into a remnant,
those far removed into a strong nation.
Then the LORD will reign over them in Mount Zion
from this time on and forever.

Psalm 46:4-11

⁴ There is a river—
its streams delight the city of God,
the holy dwelling place of the Most High.
⁵ God is within her; she will not be toppled.
God will help her when the morning dawns.
⁶ Nations rage, kingdoms topple;
the earth melts when he lifts his voice.
⁷ The LORD of Armies is with us;
the God of Jacob is our stronghold.   *Selah*

⁸ Come, see the works of the LORD,
who brings devastation on the earth.
⁹ He makes wars cease throughout the earth.
He shatters bows and cuts spears to pieces;
he sets wagons ablaze.
¹⁰ "Stop your fighting, and know that I am God,
exalted among the nations, exalted on the earth."
¹¹ The LORD of Armies is with us;
the God of Jacob is our stronghold.   *Selah*

continued

The First Noel

TEXT AND TUNE
TRADITIONAL ENGLISH CAROL

oel is the French word for Christmas, and it is rooted in the Latin word *natalis*, which means "birth." "The First Noel" is a song retelling the story of Jesus' birth. It's uncertain whether the hymn originated in French or English, but we do know it is very old, perhaps dating back to the thirteenth century. The English traditionally sang this carol on Christmas Eve while lighting and burning the Yule log, a symbol of light's victory over darkness. ❦

The first Noel the angel did say

was to certain poor shepherds in fields as they lay;

in fields where they lay keeping their sheep,

on a cold winter's night that was so deep.

Refrain:

Noel, Noel, Noel, Noel,

born is the King of Israel.

They looked up and saw a star

shining in the east, beyond them far;

and to the earth it gave great light,

and so it continued both day and night. *Refrain*

And by the light of that same star

three wise men came from country far;

to seek for a king was their intent,

and to follow the star wherever it went. *Refrain*

This star drew nigh to the northwest,

o'er Bethlehem it took its rest;

and there it did both stop and stay,

right over the place where Jesus lay. *Refrain*

Then entered in those wise men three,

full reverently upon the knee,

and offered there, in His presence,

their gold and myrrh and frankincense. *Refrain*

Isaiah 53:4-12

⁴ Yet he himself bore our sicknesses,

and he carried our pains;

but we in turn regarded him stricken,

struck down by God, and afflicted.

⁵ But he was pierced because of our rebellion,

crushed because of our iniquities;

punishment for our peace was on him,

and we are healed by his wounds.

⁶ We all went astray like sheep;

we all have turned to our own way;

and the Lord has punished him

for the iniquity of us all.

⁷ He was oppressed and afflicted,

yet he did not open his mouth.

Like a lamb led to the slaughter

and like a sheep silent before her shearers,

he did not open his mouth.

⁸ He was taken away because of oppression and judgment;

and who considered his fate?

For he was cut off from the land of the living;

he was struck because of my people's rebellion.

⁹ He was assigned a grave with the wicked,

but he was with a rich man at his death,

because he had done no violence

and had not spoken deceitfully.

¹⁰ Yet the Lord was pleased to crush him severely.

When you make him a guilt offering,

he will see his seed, he will prolong his days,

and by his hand, the Lord's pleasure will be accomplished.

¹¹ After his anguish,

he will see light and be satisfied.

By his knowledge,

my righteous servant will justify many,

and he will carry their iniquities.

¹² Therefore I will give him the many as a portion,

and he will receive the mighty as spoil,

because he willingly submitted to death,

and was counted among the rebels;

yet he bore the sin of many

and interceded for the rebels.

Myers Family Christmas Cookies

BY RAECHEL MYERS

MAKES: 12 DOZEN COOKIES

One festive afternoon every December, our extended family descends upon the Myers home—frosting spatulas in hand—to bake, decorate, and devour dozens upon dozens of Christmas cookies. When we're planning our December calendars, Cookie Day is first priority. By the end of the day, the kitchen and dining room are a glorious mess of sprinkles and flour and cookie crumb trails.

COOKIE INGREDIENTS

2 cups sugar

1 cup butter

3 eggs

1 cup evaporated milk

2 teaspoons vanilla

1 1/2 teaspoons salt

2 teaspoons baking powder

2 teaspoons baking soda

6 cups flour

FROSTING INGREDIENTS

2 pounds powdered sugar

1 cup butter flavored Crisco

1/2 cup milk

1 teaspoon vanilla

1/2 teaspoon cream of tartar

DIRECTIONS

Cream together sugar, butter, eggs, evaporated milk, vanilla, and salt.

Gradually add baking powder, baking soda, and flour to the creamed mixture.

Chill overnight – this is a must!

Preheat oven to 350°F. Roll out on a heavily floured surface and cut out cookies. Bake on a cookie sheet in the middle of the oven for 5-7 minutes, until the bottoms are very light brown.

Blend frosting ingredients and frost cooled cookies. Now get creative with toppings!

DAY

14

DATE

Grace Day

Advent is a season of anticipation and celebration. We long for the promised Savior's return, even as we rejoice that He has already come to us. Use this day to pause and reflect on this verse which describes the fullness of God the Father seen in Christ the Son.

The Word became flesh and dwelt among us. We observed his glory, the glory as the one and only Son from the Father, full of grace and truth.

JOHN 1:14

THIRD SUNDAY: DAY 15

A Prayer for
the Third Sunday of Advent

Stir up your power, O Lord, and with great might come among us; and, because we are sorely hindered by our sins, let your bountiful grace and mercy speedily help and deliver us; through Jesus Christ our Lord, to whom, with you and the Holy Spirit, be honor and glory, now and forever. Amen.

from *The Book of Common Prayer*

SCRIPTURE   Zephaniah 3:16-17

[16] On that day it will be said to Jerusalem:
"Do not fear;
Zion, do not let your hands grow weak.
[17] The Lord your God is among you,
a warrior who saves.
He will rejoice over you with gladness.
He will be quiet in his love.
He will delight in you with singing."

DECKING THE HALLS

The tradition of decorating homes with boughs of holly, mistletoe, fir trees, and other evergreens has existed for centuries. Some believe the practice began with the Romans and was adopted by Christ followers as a way of bringing nature into the home during the winter months.

Bringing greenery inside symbolized the coming renewal of life after the dormant winter. It was a reminder of the promise of resurrection. What looks dead will soon enough be green and lush and very much alive again.

The carol "Deck the Halls" may not contain overtly Christian lyrics, but it invites us into the profound Christian practice of reminding ourselves that there is life after death. It calls us to celebrate this reality together with song.

Deck the Halls

text and tune **TRADITIONAL WELSH**

Most of us aren't doing our holiday decorating in vast halls of grand houses, but no matter. "Deck the Halls" remains one of the quintessential carols sung to make merry and usher in Christmas cheer. Welsh in its inception and unknown in its authorship, the melody was originally written as the New Year's song, "Nos Galan." By 1862, hymn writer Thomas Oliphant had written and published English lyrics to accompany the tune we still use today. 🍂

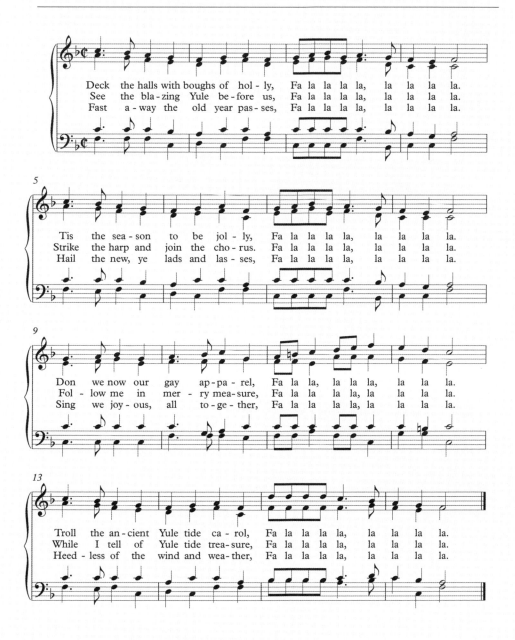

Deck the halls with boughs of hol - ly, Fa la la la la, la la la la.
See the bla - zing Yule be - fore us, Fa la la la la, la la la la.
Fast a - way the old year pas - ses, Fa la la la la, la la la la.

Tis the sea - son to be jol - ly, Fa la la la la, la la la la.
Strike the harp and join the cho - rus. Fa la la la la, la la la la.
Hail the new, ye lads and las - ses, Fa la la la la, la la la la.

Don we now our gay ap - pa - rel, Fa la la, la la la, la la la.
Fol - low me in mer - ry mea - sure, Fa la la la la, la la la la.
Sing we joy - ous, all to - ge - ther, Fa la la la la, la la la la.

Troll the an - cient Yule tide ca - rol, Fa la la la la, la la la la.
While I tell of Yule tide trea - sure, Fa la la la la, la la la la.
Heed - less of the wind and wea - ther, Fa la la la la, la la la la.

DAY

16

The Birth of John the Baptist Foretold

Luke 1:5-17

GABRIEL PREDICTS JOHN'S BIRTH

⁵ In the days of King Herod of Judea, there was a priest of Abijah's division named Zechariah. His wife was from the daughters of Aaron, and her name was Elizabeth. ⁶ Both were righteous in God's sight, living without blame according to all the commands and requirements of the Lord. ⁷ But they had no children because Elizabeth could not conceive, and both of them were well along in years.

⁸ When his division was on duty and he was serving as priest before God, ⁹ it happened that he was chosen by lot, according to the custom of the priesthood, to enter the sanctuary of the Lord and burn incense. ¹⁰ At the hour of incense the whole assembly of the people was praying outside. ¹¹ An angel of the Lord appeared to him, standing to the right of the altar of incense. ¹² When Zechariah saw him, he was terrified and overcome with fear. ¹³ But the angel said to him: "Do not be afraid, Zechariah, because your prayer has been heard. Your wife Elizabeth will bear you a son, and you will name him John. ¹⁴ There will be joy and delight for you, and many will rejoice at his birth. ¹⁵ For he will be great in the sight of the Lord and will never drink wine or beer. He will be filled with the Holy Spirit while still in his mother's womb. ¹⁶ He will turn many of the children of Israel to the Lord their God. ¹⁷ And he will go before him in the spirit and power of Elijah, to turn the hearts of fathers to their children, and the disobedient to the understanding of the righteous, to make ready for the Lord a prepared people."

Isaiah 40:1-5

GOD'S PEOPLE COMFORTED

[1] "Comfort, comfort my people,"
says your God.
[2] "Speak tenderly to Jerusalem,
and announce to her
that her time of forced labor is over,
her iniquity has been pardoned,
and she has received from the LORD's hand
double for all her sins."

[3] A voice of one crying out:

Prepare the way of the LORD in the wilderness;
make a straight highway for our God in the desert.
[4] Every valley will be lifted up,
and every mountain and hill will be leveled;
the uneven ground will become smooth
and the rough places, a plain.
[5] And the glory of the LORD will appear,
and all humanity together will see it,
for the mouth of the LORD has spoken.

Malachi 3:1-4

[1] "See, I am going to send my messenger, and he will clear the way before me. Then the Lord you seek will suddenly come to his temple, the Messenger of the covenant you delight in—see, he is coming," says the LORD of Armies. [2] But who can endure the day of his coming? And who will be able to stand when he appears? For he will be like a refiner's fire and like launderer's bleach. [3] He will be like a refiner and purifier of silver; he will purify the sons of Levi and refine them like gold and silver. Then they will present offerings to the LORD in righteousness. [4] And the offerings of Judah and Jerusalem will please the LORD as in days of old and years gone by.

Mark 1:1-8

THE MESSIAH'S HERALD

[1] The beginning of the gospel of Jesus Christ, the Son of God. [2] As it is written in Isaiah the prophet:

See, I am sending my messenger ahead of you;
he will prepare your way.
[3] A voice of one crying out in the wilderness:
Prepare the way for the Lord;
make his paths straight!

[4] John came baptizing in the wilderness and proclaiming a baptism of repentance for the forgiveness of sins. [5] The whole Judean countryside and all the people of Jerusalem were going out to him, and they were baptized by him in the Jordan River, confessing their sins. [6] John wore a camel-hair garment with a leather belt around his waist and ate locusts and wild honey.

[7] He proclaimed,

"One who is more powerful than I am is coming after me.

I am not worthy to stoop down and untie the strap of his sandals. [8] I baptize you with water, but he will baptize you with the Holy Spirit."

DATE

NOTES

CHRISTMAS TRADITIONS

XMAS

Why is Christmas sometimes spelled "Xmas"? The "X" actually refers directly to Christ. It is the first letter of the Greek word Χριστός, or *Christos*, which means "anointed one." The letter gave early Christians a way to communicate with one another while under threat of persecution. The invention of Gutenberg's printing press in 1436 helped standardize the abbreviation. Since switching out the movable type was tedious and expensive, substituting the word Christ with an "X" cut the printing costs of church publications.

Zechariah Struck Silent

Luke 1:18-25

18 "How can I know this?" Zechariah asked the angel. "For I am an old man, and my wife is well along in years."

19 The angel answered him, "I am Gabriel, who stands in the presence of God, and I was sent to speak to you and tell you this good news. 20 Now listen. You will become silent and unable to speak until the day these things take place, because you did not believe my words, which will be fulfilled in their proper time."

21 Meanwhile, the people were waiting for Zechariah, amazed that he stayed so long in the sanctuary. 22 When he did come out, he could not speak to them. Then they realized that he had seen a vision in the sanctuary. He was making signs to them and remained speechless. 23 When the days of his ministry were completed, he went back home.

24 After these days his wife Elizabeth conceived and kept herself in seclusion for five months. She said,

25 "The Lord has done this for me.

He has looked with favor in these days to take away my disgrace among the people."

Genesis 18:9-15

SARAH LAUGHS

[9] "Where is your wife Sarah?" they asked him.

"There, in the tent," he answered.

[10] The LORD said, "I will certainly come back to you in about a year's time, and your wife Sarah will have a son!" Now Sarah was listening at the entrance of the tent behind him.

[11] Abraham and Sarah were old and getting on in years. Sarah had passed the age of childbearing. [12] So she laughed to herself: "After I am worn out and my lord is old, will I have delight?"

[13] But the LORD asked Abraham, "Why did Sarah laugh, saying, 'Can I really have a baby when I'm old?' [14] Is anything impossible for the LORD? At the appointed time I will come back to you, and in about a year she will have a son."

[15] Sarah denied it. "I did not laugh," she said, because she was afraid.

But he replied, "No, you did laugh."

Luke 7:18-28

IN PRAISE OF JOHN THE BAPTIST

[18] Then John's disciples told him about all these things. So John summoned two of his disciples [19] and sent them to the Lord, asking, "Are you the one who is to come, or should we expect someone else?"

[20] When the men reached him, they said, "John the Baptist sent us to ask you, 'Are you the one who is to come, or should we expect someone else?'"

[21] At that time Jesus healed many people of diseases, afflictions, and evil spirits, and he granted sight to many blind people. [22] He replied to them, "Go and report to John what you have seen and heard: The blind receive their sight, the lame walk, those with leprosy are cleansed, the deaf hear, the dead are raised, and the poor are told the good news, [23] and blessed is the one who isn't offended by me."

[24] After John's messengers left, he began to speak to the crowds about John: "What did you go out into the wilderness to see? A reed swaying in the wind? [25] What then did you go out to see? A man dressed in soft clothes? See, those who are splendidly dressed and live in luxury are in royal palaces. [26] What then did you go out to see? A prophet? Yes, I tell you, and more than a prophet. [27] This is the one about whom it is written:

See, I am sending my messenger
ahead of you;
he will prepare your way before you.

[28] I tell you, among those born of women no one is greater than John, but the least in the kingdom of God is greater than he."

Romans 4:19-21

[19] He did not weaken in faith when he considered his own body to be already dead (since he was about a hundred years old) and also the deadness of Sarah's womb. [20] He did not waver in unbelief at God's promise but was strengthened in his faith and gave glory to God, [21] because he was fully convinced that what God had promised, he was also able to do.

DATE

NOTES

DAY

18

The Angel Visits Mary and Joseph

Luke 1:26-38

GABRIEL PREDICTS JESUS'S BIRTH

²⁶ In the sixth month, the angel Gabriel was sent by God to a town in Galilee called Nazareth, ²⁷ to a virgin engaged to a man named Joseph, of the house of David. The virgin's name was Mary. ²⁸ And the angel came to her and said, "Greetings, favored woman! The Lord is with you." ²⁹ But she was deeply troubled by this statement, wondering what kind of greeting this could be. ³⁰ Then the angel told her: "Do not be afraid, Mary, for you have found favor with God. ³¹ Now listen: You will conceive and give birth to a son, and you will name him Jesus. ³² He will be great and will be called the Son of the Most High, and the Lord God will give him the throne of his father David. ³³ He will reign over the house of Jacob forever, and his kingdom will have no end."

³⁴ Mary asked the angel, "How can this be, since I have not had sexual relations with a man?"

³⁵ The angel replied to her: "The Holy Spirit will come upon you, and the power of the Most High will overshadow you. Therefore, the holy one to be born will be called the Son of God. ³⁶ And consider your relative Elizabeth—even she has conceived a son in her old age, and this is the sixth month for her who was called childless. ³⁷ For nothing will be impossible with God."

³⁸ "I am the Lord's servant," said Mary. "May it be done to me according to your word." Then the angel left her.

continued

O Come, O Come, Immanuel

TEXT LATIN, 12TH CENTURY
TUNE THOMAS HELMORE, 1854

John Mason Neale was a British hymn writer, scholar, and Anglican. As a Christ follower, he spent much of his life dedicated to the hope of reconciliation and unity between the Catholic and Anglican Churches. His calling brought him both praise and persecution, but his hymn writing left a lasting impact on the Church. Neale is credited with writing songs such as "Good Christian Men Rejoice" and "Good King Wenceslas," and in 1851, "O Come, O Come, Immanuel," which he adapted and translated from Latin into English and set to a melody reminiscent of Gregorian chant. ❦

O come, O come, Immanuel,

and ransom captive Israel

that mourns in lonely exile here

until the Son of God appears.

Refrain:

Rejoice! Rejoice! Immanuel

shall come to you, O Israel.

O come, O Wisdom from on high,

who ordered all things mightily

to us the path of knowledge show

and teach us in its ways to go. *Refrain*

O come, O come, great Lord of might,

who to Your tribes on Sinai's height

in ancient times did give the law

in cloud and majesty and awe. *Refrain*

O come, O Branch of Jesse's stem,

unto Your own and rescue them!

From depths of hell Your people save,

and give them victory o'er the grave. *Refrain*

Matthew 1:18-25

THE NATIVITY OF THE CHRIST

¹⁸ The birth of Jesus Christ came about this way: After his mother Mary had been engaged to Joseph, it was discovered before they came together that she was pregnant from the Holy Spirit. ¹⁹ So her husband Joseph, being a righteous man, and not wanting to disgrace her publicly, decided to divorce her secretly.

²⁰ But after he had considered these things, an angel of the Lord appeared to him in a dream, saying, "Joseph, son of David, don't be afraid to take Mary as your wife, because what has been conceived in her is from the Holy Spirit.

²¹ She will give birth to a son, and you are to name him Jesus, because he will save his people from their sins."

²² Now all this took place to fulfill what was spoken by the Lord through the prophet:

²³ See, the virgin will become pregnant
and give birth to a son,
and they will name him Immanuel,

which is translated "God is with us."

²⁴ When Joseph woke up, he did as the Lord's angel had commanded him. He married her ²⁵ but did not have sexual relations with her until she gave birth to a son. And he named him Jesus.

Job 33:4

The Spirit of God has made me,
and the breath of the Almighty gives me life.

DATE

NOTES

1 Joseph and Mary leave their home in Nazareth to register for Caesar's census in Bethlehem.

LUKE 2:1-5

2 Mary gives birth to Jesus in Bethlehem.

LUKE 2:6-7

3 After the 40 days of purification prescribed in the law of Moses (Leviticus 12), Mary and Joseph take Jesus to Jerusalem to present Him to God in the temple.

LUKE 2:21-35

4 Joseph, Mary, and baby Jesus return to Bethlehem. During this time, magi from the east come looking for the one born king of the Jews.

MATTHEW 2:1-12

5 Joseph and Mary flee to Egypt after the angel of the Lord warns them of Herod's plan to kill Jesus.

MATTHEW 2:13-18

6 After Herod's death, Joseph, Mary, and Jesus return to Israel to live in Nazareth.

MATTHEW 2:19-23

Nile River

Mediterranean Sea

5 | EGYPT

EGYPT

Red Sea

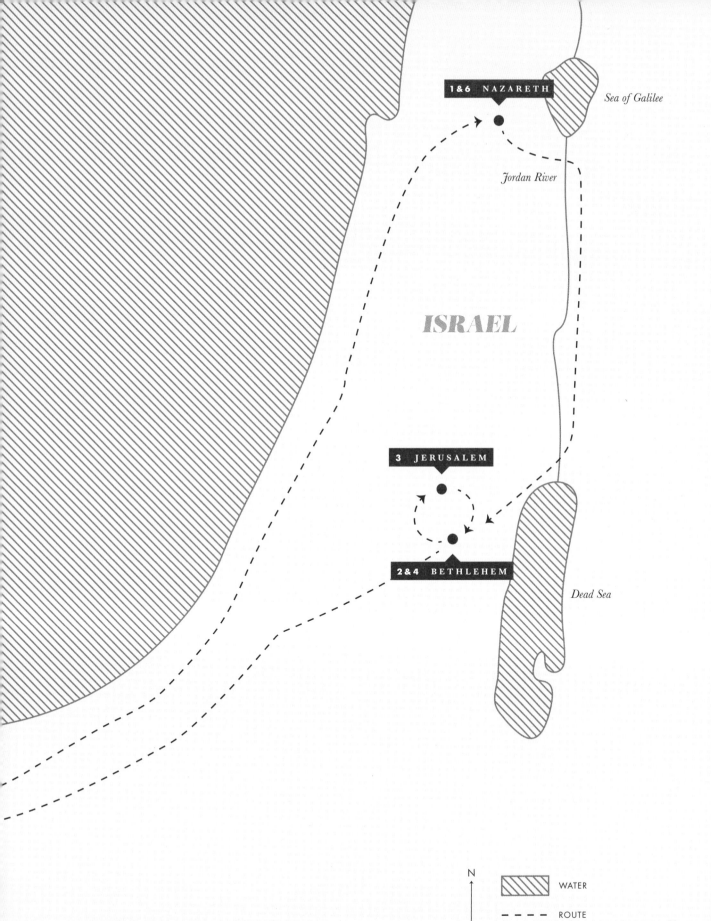

1&6 NAZARETH

Sea of Galilee

Jordan River

ISRAEL

3 JERUSALEM

2&4 BETHLEHEM

Dead Sea

N

WATER

ROUTE

DAY

19

Mary Visits Elizabeth

Luke 1:39-55

MARY'S VISIT TO ELIZABETH

³⁹ In those days Mary set out and hurried to a town in the hill country of Judah ⁴⁰ where she entered Zechariah's house and greeted Elizabeth. ⁴¹ When Elizabeth heard Mary's greeting, the baby leaped inside her, and Elizabeth was filled with the Holy Spirit. ⁴² Then she exclaimed with a loud cry: "Blessed are you among women, and your child will be blessed! ⁴³ How could this happen to me, that the mother of my Lord should come to me? ⁴⁴ For you see, when the sound of your greeting reached my ears, the baby leaped for joy inside me. ⁴⁵ Blessed is she who has believed that the Lord would fulfill what he has spoken to her!"

MARY'S PRAISE

⁴⁶ And Mary said:

My soul praises the greatness of the Lord,
⁴⁷ and my spirit rejoices in God my Savior,
⁴⁸ because he has looked with favor
on the humble condition of his servant.

Surely, from now on all generations will call me blessed,

⁴⁹ because the Mighty One
has done great things for me,
and his name is holy.
⁵⁰ His mercy is from generation to generation
on those who fear him.
⁵¹ He has done a mighty deed with his arm;
he has scattered the proud
because of the thoughts of their hearts;
⁵² he has toppled the mighty from their thrones
and exalted the lowly.
⁵³ He has satisfied the hungry with good things
and sent the rich away empty.
⁵⁴ He has helped his servant Israel,
remembering his mercy
⁵⁵ to Abraham and his descendants forever,
just as he spoke to our ancestors.

Genesis 25:21-26

[21] Isaac prayed to the LORD on behalf of his wife because she was childless. The LORD was receptive to his prayer, and his wife Rebekah conceived. [22] But the children inside her struggled with each other, and she said, "Why is this happening to me?" So she went to inquire of the LORD. [23] And the LORD said to her:

> Two nations are in your womb;
> two peoples will come from you and be separated.
> One people will be stronger than the other,
> and the older will serve the younger.

[24] When her time came to give birth, there were indeed twins in her womb. [25] The first one came out red-looking, covered with hair like a fur coat, and they named him Esau. [26] After this, his brother came out grasping Esau's heel with his hand. So he was named Jacob. Isaac was sixty years old when they were born.

John 4:24

God is spirit, and those who worship him must worship in Spirit and in truth.

DATE

NOTES

CHRISTMAS TRADITIONS

NATIVITY SCENES

How long have nativity scenes been around?
The first known nativity scenes date back to tenth century Rome, but many credit St. Francis of Assisi with solidifying the practice in 1223. That year, Francis held the Christ's Mass service by candlelight in a nearby cave. There he arranged a manger filled with straw and surrounded it with real animals. When the townspeople came for the service, they were greatly moved by the recreation of the scene of Christ's birth. The idea caught on and continues all around the world to this day.

DAY

20

The Birth of John the Baptist

Luke 1:57-80

THE BIRTH AND NAMING OF JOHN

⁵⁷ Now the time had come for Elizabeth to give birth, and she had a son. ⁵⁸ Then her neighbors and relatives heard that the Lord had shown her his great mercy, and they rejoiced with her.

⁵⁹ When they came to circumcise the child on the eighth day, they were going to name him Zechariah, after his father. ⁶⁰ But his mother responded, "No. He will be called John."

⁶¹ Then they said to her, "None of your relatives has that name." ⁶² So they motioned to his father to find out what he wanted him to be called. ⁶³ He asked for a writing tablet and wrote: "His name is John." And they were all amazed. ⁶⁴ Immediately his mouth was opened and his tongue set free, and he began to speak, praising God. ⁶⁵ Fear came on all those who lived around them, and all these things were being talked about throughout the hill country of Judea. ⁶⁶ All who heard about him took it to heart, saying, "What then will this child become?" For, indeed, the Lord's hand was with him.

ZECHARIAH'S PROPHECY

⁶⁷ Then his father Zechariah was filled with the Holy Spirit and prophesied:

⁶⁸ Blessed is the Lord, the God of Israel,
because he has visited
and provided redemption for his people.
⁶⁹ He has raised up a horn of salvation for us
in the house of his servant David,
⁷⁰ just as he spoke by the mouth
of his holy prophets in ancient times;
⁷¹ salvation from our enemies
and from the hand of those who hate us.
⁷² He has dealt mercifully with our fathers
and remembered his holy covenant—
⁷³ the oath that he swore to our father Abraham.
He has given us the privilege,
⁷⁴ since we have been rescued
from the hand of our enemies,
to serve him without fear
⁷⁵ in holiness and righteousness
in his presence all our days.

⁷⁶ And you, child,
will be called
a prophet of the
Most High,

for you will go before the Lord
to prepare his ways,
⁷⁷ to give his people knowledge of salvation
through the forgiveness of their sins.
⁷⁸ Because of our God's merciful compassion,
the dawn from on high will visit us
⁷⁹ to shine on those who live in darkness
and the shadow of death,
to guide our feet into the way of peace.

⁸⁰ The child grew up and became spiritually strong, and he was in the wilderness until the day of his public appearance to Israel.

DATE

NOTES

Photos by Amanda Barnhart

Rosemary and Garlic Roast Beef

BY THE SHE READS TRUTH TEAM

SERVES: 6-8

Christmas is a feasting season, and nothing says "feast" like a rich and hearty main course. We love this recipe because it looks and tastes like something technically advanced, but it's actually very simple. One of our favorite steps, from an artistic perspective, is the pan searing at the beginning. Think of it as starting with the end in mind—a chance to art direct your meal well before the guests arrive.

INGREDIENTS

3 pound boneless ribeye roast

1/4 cup fresh rosemary or other favorite herbs, chopped

1/4 cup garlic (about 20 cloves), chopped

Salt and freshly ground pepper

4 tablespoons olive oil, divided

4 tablespoons butter, divided

4 cups of a variety of mushrooms, sliced to about the same size

1 cup beef stock

DIRECTIONS

Preheat oven to 350°F.

Combine rosemary, garlic, and 2 tablespoons olive oil. Set aside.

Season ribeye liberally on all sides with salt and pepper, then use kitchen twine to tie the roast.

Heat the remaining olive oil over medium heat in a cast iron skillet or oven-safe pan. Once the oil is hot, sear all sides of the meat.

Carefully remove skillet from heat and coat the roast with the rosemary-garlic mixture.

Cook uncovered for 1 to 1 1/2 hours, or until a meat thermometer reads 135°F. Let the roast rest outside the cast iron skillet for at least ten minutes. For a medium rare roast, the final temperature should be 145°F.

While the roast is resting, sauté the mushrooms over medium heat in the empty roast skillet with 2 tablespoons butter until cooked through and no liquid is left in the pan, about 5 minutes. Season with salt and pepper to taste.

Set mushrooms aside in a bowl. Add stock to the skillet and deglaze, scraping all the bits from the bottom. Let simmer until sauce thickens.

Add the mushrooms to the sauce, stirring in the remaining butter, until sauce is silky. Place the roast back in the cast iron or on a serving platter, and spoon the sauce over the roast.

Garnish with remaining fresh rosemary.

Yorkshire Pudding Popovers

BY RAECHEL MYERS

SERVES: 12 MUFFIN-SIZED POPOVERS OR 6 LARGER POPOVERS

I'm a bit of a late arrival to the Yorkshire Pudding party, which probably explains why I was caught off guard when they tasted less like a donut and more like a quiche. Like most baked goods, Yorkshire Pudding is a science experiment every time, which makes it extra exciting. Will they "pop over"? Will they flop? Either way, this traditional English side is destined for holiday greatness when served alongside our Rosemary and Garlic Roast Beef.

INGREDIENTS

6 tablespoons salted butter, melted

1 cup all-purpose flour

3 large eggs

1 cup milk

Salt and pepper

DIRECTIONS

Preheat oven to 425°F.

Brush the melted butter generously in and around each hole of a 12-hole nonstick muffin or popover pan, all the way up to the top.

Place the pan in the oven for a minute or two to heat the butter. Don't leave it in too long!

To make the batter, add the flour to a bowl and stir in the eggs and milk until smooth. Lightly season with salt and pepper.

Remove the heated tray from the oven and carefully distribute the batter evenly among the 12 cups.

Bake 20-25 minutes, or until the puddings have puffed up and turned a beautiful golden brown.

Serve piping hot with a roast or other cold-weather meal.

DAY

21

Grace Day

Advent is a season of anticipation and celebration. We long for the promised Savior's return, even as we rejoice that He has already come to us. Use this day to pause and reflect on this verse from Zechariah's prophecy in Luke about the Lord's promise to redeem His people.

Blessed is the Lord, the God of Israel, because he has visited and provided redemption for his people.

LUKE 1:68

*Christmas
Week*

Let Every
Heart
Prepare
Him Room

A Prayer for the Fourth Sunday of Advent

Purify our conscience, Almighty God, by your daily visitation, that your Son Jesus Christ, at His coming, may find in us a mansion prepared for Himself; who lives and reigns with you, in the unity of the Holy Spirit, one God, now and forever. Amen.

from *The Book of Common Prayer*

SCRIPTURE

Psalm 51:1-2, 7

A PRAYER FOR RESTORATION

[1] Be gracious to me, God,
according to your faithful love;
according to your abundant compassion,
blot out my rebellion.
[2] Completely wash away my guilt
and cleanse me from my sin.

[7] Purify me with hyssop, and I will be clean;
wash me, and I will be whiter than snow.

Silent Night! Holy Night!

text JOSEPH MOHR
tune FRANZ GRUBER

On Christmas Eve 1818, the hymn we call "Silent Night" was born. A Catholic priest named Joseph Mohr wanted to write something to celebrate and reflect on the Christmas season, and so he wrote the lyrics to the song "Stille Nacht" (German for "Silent Night") from his tiny village in the Swiss Alps. The local church organist, Franz Gruber, composed a melody to match Mohr's verse. That very night the carol was sung for the first time during the midnight Christmas mass. ♆

1 Si - lent night, ho - ly night! All is calm, all is bright
2 Si - lent night, ho - ly night! Shep - herds quake at the sight,
3 Si - lent night, ho - ly night! Son of God, love's pure light,

'round yon vir - gin mo - ther and child; ho - ly in - fant, so ten - der and
glo - ries stream— from hea - ven a - far, heaven - ly hosts— sing al - le - lu -
ra - diant beams— from Thy ho - ly face, with the dawn of re - deem - ing

mild, sleep in hea - ven - ly peace,— sleep— in hea - ven - ly peace.
ia; Christ, the Sa - vior, is born!— Christ, the Sa - vior, is born!
grace, Je - sus, Lord, at Thy birth,— Je - sus, Lord, at Thy birth.

DAY

23

The Birth of Jesus

A PRAYER FOR THE NATIVITY OF OUR LORD: CHRISTMAS DAY

Almighty God, you have given your only begotten Son to take our nature upon Him, and to be born this day of a pure virgin: Grant that we, who have been born again and made your children by adoption and grace, may daily be renewed by your Holy Spirit; through our Lord Jesus Christ, to whom with you and the same Spirit be honor and glory, now and forever. Amen.

from *The Book of Common Prayer*

SCRIPTURE

Luke 2:1-20

THE BIRTH OF JESUS

[1] In those days a decree went out from Caesar Augustus that the whole empire should be registered. [2] This first registration took place while Quirinius was governing Syria. [3] So everyone went to be registered, each to his own town.

[4] Joseph also went up from the town of Nazareth in Galilee, to Judea, to the city of David, which is called Bethlehem, because he was of the house and family line of David, [5] to be registered along with Mary, who was engaged to him and was pregnant. [6] While they were there, the time came for her to give birth.

[7] Then she gave birth to her firstborn Son, and she wrapped him tightly in cloth and laid him in a manger,

because there was no guest room available for them.

THE SHEPHERDS AND THE ANGELS

[8] In the same region, shepherds were staying out in the fields and keeping watch at night over their flock. [9] Then an angel of the Lord stood before them, and the glory of the Lord shone around them, and they were terrified. [10] But the angel said to them, "Don't be afraid, for look, I proclaim to you good news of great joy that will be for all the people: [11] Today in the city of David a Savior was born for you, who is the Messiah, the Lord. [12] This will be the sign for you: You will find a baby wrapped tightly in cloth and lying in a manger."

[13] Suddenly there was a multitude of the heavenly host with the angel, praising God and saying:

> [14] Glory to God in the highest heaven,
> and peace on earth to people he favors!

[15] When the angels had left them and returned to heaven, the shepherds said to one another, "Let's go straight to Bethlehem and see what has happened, which the Lord has made known to us."

[16] They hurried off and found both Mary and Joseph, and the baby who was lying in the manger. [17] After seeing them, they reported the message they were told about this child, [18] and all who heard it were amazed at what the shepherds said to them. [19] But Mary was treasuring up all these things in her heart and meditating on them. [20] The shepherds returned, glorifying and praising God for all the things they had seen and heard, which were just as they had been told.

Galatians 4:1-7

[1] Now I say that as long as the heir is a child, he differs in no way from a slave, though he is the owner of everything. [2] Instead, he is under guardians and trustees until the time set by his father. [3] In the same way we also, when we were children, were in slavery under the elements of the world. [4] When the time came to completion, God sent his Son, born of a woman, born under the law, [5] to redeem those under the law, so that we might receive adoption as sons. [6] And because you are sons, God sent the Spirit of his Son into our hearts, crying, "Abba, Father!" [7] So you are no longer a slave but a son, and if a son, then God has made you an heir.

DATE

NOTES

Angels We Have Heard on High

text and tune
FRENCH CAROL, 18TH CENTURY

It was once the custom of French shepherds to call out to one another on Christmas Eve, "Gloria in excelsis Deo, gloria in excelsis Deo," or "Glory to God in the highest." The call signified the same proclamation made by the heavenly hosts on the night Jesus was born (Luke 2:14). The French shepherds most likely utilized a Latin song to accompany those verses from Scripture—a song which happens to include the refrain, "Angels we have heard on high." The melody we sing today at Christmastime originated in the eighteenth century, but lyric and melody were not published together until 1855. ❦

1 An - gels we have heard on high sweet - ly sing - ing o'er the plains,
2 Shep - herds, why this ju - bi - lee? Why your joy - ous strains pro - long?
3 Come to Beth - le - hem, and see Him whose birth the an - gels sing;

and the moun - tains in re - ply e - cho back their joy - ous strains.
Say, what may the ti - dings be which in - spire your heaven - ly song?
come, a - dore on ben - ded knee Christ the Lord, the new - born King.

Glo - - - - - - - - ri - a

in ex - cel - sis De - o! Glo - - - - -

- - - ri - a in ex - cel - sis De - o!

The Wise Men Visit the Christ Child

Matthew 2:1-23

WISE MEN VISIT THE KING

¹ After Jesus was born in Bethlehem of Judea in the days of King Herod, wise men from the east arrived in Jerusalem, ² saying, "Where is he who has been born king of the Jews? For we saw his star at its rising and have come to worship him."

³ When King Herod heard this, he was deeply disturbed, and all Jerusalem with him. ⁴ So he assembled all the chief priests and scribes of the people and asked them where the Christ would be born.

⁵ "In Bethlehem of Judea," they told him, "because this is what was written by the prophet:

⁶ And you, Bethlehem, in the land of Judah,
are by no means least among the rulers of Judah:
Because out of you will come a ruler
who will shepherd my people Israel."

⁷ Then Herod secretly summoned the wise men and asked them the exact time the star appeared. ⁸ He sent them to Bethlehem and said, "Go and search carefully for the child. When you find him, report back to me so that I too can go and worship him."

⁹ After hearing the king, they went on their way. And there it was—the star they had seen at its rising. It led them until it came and stopped above the place where the child was. ¹⁰ When they saw the star, they were overwhelmed with joy. ¹¹ Entering the house, they saw the child with Mary

his mother, and falling to their knees, they worshiped him. Then they opened their treasures and presented him with gifts: gold, frankincense, and myrrh. [12] And being warned in a dream not to go back to Herod, they returned to their own country by another route.

THE FLIGHT INTO EGYPT

[13] After they were gone, an angel of the Lord appeared to Joseph in a dream, saying, "Get up! Take the child and his mother, flee to Egypt, and stay there until I tell you. For Herod is about to search for the child to kill him." [14] So he got up, took the child and his mother during the night, and escaped to Egypt. [15] He stayed there until Herod's death, so that what was spoken by the Lord through the prophet might be fulfilled: Out of Egypt I called my Son.

THE MASSACRE OF THE INNOCENTS

[16] Then Herod, when he realized that he had been outwitted by the wise men, flew into a rage. He gave orders to massacre all the boys in and around Bethlehem who were two years old and under, in keeping with the time he had learned from the wise men. [17] Then what was spoken through Jeremiah the prophet was fulfilled:

[18] A voice was heard in Ramah,
weeping, and great mourning,
Rachel weeping for her children;
and she refused to be consoled,
because they are no more.

THE RETURN TO NAZARETH

[19] After Herod died, an angel of the Lord appeared in a dream to Joseph in Egypt, [20] saying, "Get up, take the child and his mother, and go to the land of Israel, because those who intended to kill the child are dead." [21] So he got up, took the child and his mother, and entered the land of Israel. [22] But when he heard that Archelaus was ruling over Judea in place of his father Herod, he was afraid to go there. And being warned in a dream, he withdrew to the region of Galilee. [23] Then he went and settled in a town called Nazareth to fulfill what was spoken through the prophets, that he would be called a Nazarene.

Jeremiah 31:15-20

[15] This is what the LORD says:

A voice was heard in Ramah,
a lament with bitter weeping—
Rachel weeping for her children,
refusing to be comforted for her children
because they are no more.

[16] This is what the LORD says:

Keep your voice from weeping
and your eyes from tears,
for the reward for your work will come—
this is the LORD's declaration—
and your children will return from the enemy's land.
[17] There is hope for your future—
this is the LORD's declaration—
and your children will return to their own territory.
[18] I have surely heard Ephraim moaning,
"You disciplined me, and I have been disciplined
like an untrained calf.

Take me back, so that I can return, for you, LORD, are my God.

[19] After my return, I felt regret;
After I was instructed, I struck my thigh in grief.
I was ashamed and humiliated
because I bore the disgrace of my youth."
[20] Isn't Ephraim a precious son to me,
a delightful child?
Whenever I speak against him,
I certainly still think about him.
Therefore, my inner being yearns for him;
I will truly have compassion on him.
This is the LORD's declaration.

DATE

NOTES

Gold, Frankincense, and Myrrh

If you're familiar with the Christmas story, you've heard of the wise men, or "magi" from the east, described in Matthew 2. These men set off on a journey in search of the Christ Child so they could present Him with gifts. The precise number of magi who visited Jesus is unclear. They are often called the "Three Wise Men" becuase they brought three gifts: gold, frankincense, and myrrh.

Each of these gifts was quite costly at the time, leading scholars to believe the men bearing them must have been wealthy themselves, perhaps even kings. But aside from the monetary value, each of these gifts carried a symbolic—some might even say prophetic—significance.

The gifts of gold and frankincense speak to Jesus' role as the everlasting King and Priest of God's people, and the myrrh prophetically points to His death, burial, resurrection, and victory over sin and the grave. ❧

GOLD
Gold represented royalty or kingship, and in Christ's case, His divinity.

FRANKINCENSE
Frankincense was a perfumed oil regularly used by priests during religious ceremonies. This gift anticipated that Jesus, though not born into the line of priests, would become our High Priest.

MYRRH
Myrrh, another perfumed oil, was the most precious of the three gifts. Worth five times the value of gold, myrrh was often used in funerals and burial services. This might seem an unusual gift to give a child, but many believe it foreshadowed Jesus' own sacrificial death on the cross. In John 19, Nicodemus prepared Jesus' body for burial by using "a mixture of about seventy-five pounds of myrrh and aloes" (v.39).

DAY

25

Jesus Presented in the Temple

Luke 2:21-40

THE CIRCUMCISION AND PRESENTATION OF JESUS

²¹ When the eight days were completed for his circumcision, he was named Jesus—the name given by the angel before he was conceived. ²² And when the days of their purification according to the law of Moses were finished, they brought him up to Jerusalem to present him to the Lord ²³ (just as it is written in the law of the Lord, Every firstborn male will be dedicated to the Lord) ²⁴ and to offer a sacrifice (according to what is stated in the law of the Lord, a pair of turtledoves or two young pigeons).

SIMEON'S PROPHETIC PRAISE

²⁵ There was a man in Jerusalem whose name was Simeon. This man was righteous and devout, looking forward to Israel's consolation, and the Holy Spirit was on him. ²⁶ It had been revealed to him by the Holy Spirit that he would not see death before he saw the Lord's Messiah. ²⁷ Guided by the Spirit, he entered the temple. When the parents brought in the child Jesus to perform for him what was customary under the law, ²⁸ Simeon took him up in his arms, praised God, and said,

²⁹ Now, Master,
you can dismiss your servant in peace,
as you promised.
³⁰ For my eyes have seen your salvation.
³¹ You have prepared it
in the presence of all peoples—
³² a light for revelation to the Gentiles
and glory to your people Israel.

³³ His father and mother were amazed at what was being said about him. ³⁴ Then Simeon blessed them and told his mother Mary: "Indeed, this child is destined to cause the fall and rise of many in Israel and to be a sign that will be opposed— ³⁵ and a sword will pierce your own soul—that the thoughts of many hearts may be revealed."

ANNA'S TESTIMONY

³⁶ There was also a prophetess, Anna, a daughter of Phanuel, of the tribe of Asher. She was well along in years, having lived with her husband seven years after

her marriage, [37] and was a widow for eighty-four years. She did not leave the temple, serving God night and day with fasting and prayers. [38] At that very moment, she came up and began to thank God and to speak about him to all who were looking forward to the redemption of Jerusalem.

THE FAMILY'S RETURN TO NAZARETH

[39] When they had completed everything according to the law of the Lord, they returned to Galilee, to their own town of Nazareth.

[40] The boy grew up and became strong, filled with wisdom, and God's grace was on him.

Leviticus 12:1-8

PURIFICATION AFTER CHILDBIRTH

[1] The LORD spoke to Moses: [2] "Tell the Israelites: When a woman becomes pregnant and gives birth to a male child, she will be unclean seven days, as she is during the days of her menstrual impurity. [3] The flesh of his foreskin must be circumcised on the eighth day. [4] She will continue in purification from her bleeding for thirty-three days. She must not touch any holy thing or go into the sanctuary until completing her days of purification. [5] But if she gives birth to a female child, she will be unclean for two weeks as she is during her menstrual impurity. She will continue in purification from her bleeding for sixty-six days.

[6] "When her days of purification are complete, whether for a son or daughter, she is to bring to the priest at the entrance to the tent of meeting a year-old male lamb for a burnt offering, and a young pigeon or a turtledove for a sin offering. [7] He will present them before the LORD and make atonement on her behalf; she will be clean from her discharge of blood. This is the law for a woman giving birth, whether to a male or female. [8] But if she doesn't have sufficient means for a sheep, she may take two turtledoves or two young pigeons, one for a burnt offering and the other for a sin offering. Then the priest will make atonement on her behalf, and she will be clean."

DATE

NOTES

The Twelve Days of Christmas

THE HISTORY

You've heard the song, but what exactly are the Twelve Days of Christmas? The Twelve Days of Christmas, also known as Christmastide or Twelve-tide, is a season during which many Christian traditions celebrate the events of the nativity of Jesus. The celebration begins on Christmas Day (the first day of Christmas) and culminates twelve days later on the evening of January 5, also known as Twelfth Night (which commemorates the visit of the magi).

THE SONG

The song is sung from the perspective of someone who is being showered with gifts from their true love. When calculating the number of gifts given in the song, many make the mistake of thinking it is 78 total: one partridge in a pear tree, two turtledoves, three french hens, and so on. Actually, the beloved receives 364 gifts, one for each day of the year except Christmas Eve, which is a day of anticipation.

THE COST

From the PNC Financial Services Group:

"For more than 30 years, PNC has calculated the prices of the twelve gifts from the classic carol 'The Twelve Days of Christmas.' The result is the PNC Christmas Price Index, a unique and whimsical holiday tradition that makes learning about the economy fun."

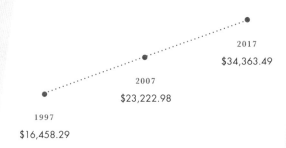

2017
$34,363.49

2007
$23,222.98

1997
$16,458.29

The Cost of Christmas, 1997-2017

DAY	GIFT	DAILY GIFT TOTAL
1	**A PARTRIDGE IN A PEAR TREE**	1
2	*The previous day's gifts, plus* **TWO TURTLEDOVES**	3
3	*The previous day's gifts, plus* **THREE FRENCH HENS**	6
4	*The previous day's gifts, plus* **FOUR CALLING BIRDS**	10
5	*The previous day's gifts, plus* **FIVE GOLDEN RINGS**	15
6	*The previous day's gifts, plus* **SIX GEESE A-LAYING**	21
7	*The previous day's gifts, plus* **SEVEN SWANS A-SWIMMING**	28
8	*The previous day's gifts, plus* **EIGHT MAIDS A-MILKING**	36
9	*The previous day's gifts, plus* **NINE LADIES DANCING**	45
10	*The previous day's gifts, plus* **TEN LORDS A-LEAPING**	55
11	*The previous day's gifts, plus* **ELEVEN PIPERS PIPING**	66
12	*The previous day's gifts, plus* **TWELVE DRUMMERS DRUMMING**	78

TOTAL GIFTS

364

CHRISTMAS TRADITIONS

BELLS

How did bells become a symbol of the Christmas season? Bells have long been used as a means of quick communication throughout various cultures. Bells may toll slowly and steadily to grieve someone's death, or sound an intricate pattern (known as change-ringing) to announce a newly wedded couple's bliss. The pealing of bells at midnight on Christmas Eve proclaims the arrival of Jesus Christ, the Messiah.

DAY

26

Seek the Lord While He May Be Found

Isaiah 55:6-13

⁶ Seek the LORD while he may be found;
call to him while he is near.
⁷ Let the wicked one abandon his way
and the sinful one his thoughts;
let him return to the LORD,
so he may have compassion on him,
and to our God, for he will freely forgive.

⁸ "For my thoughts are not your thoughts,
and your ways are not my ways."

    This is the LORD's declaration.
⁹ "For as heaven is higher than earth,
so my ways are higher than your ways,
and my thoughts than your thoughts.
¹⁰ For just as rain and snow fall from heaven
and do not return there
without saturating the earth
and making it germinate and sprout,
and providing seed to sow
and food to eat,

¹¹ so my word that comes from my mouth
will not return to me empty,
but it will accomplish what I please
and will prosper in what I send it to do."

¹² You will indeed go out with joy
and be peacefully guided;
the mountains and the hills will break into singing before you,
and all the trees of the field will clap their hands.
¹³ Instead of the thornbush, a cypress will come up,
and instead of the brier, a myrtle will come up;
this will stand as a monument for the LORD,
an everlasting sign that will not be destroyed.

Hebrews 1:3

The Son is the radiance of God's glory and the exact expression
of his nature, sustaining all things by his powerful word. After
making purification for sins, he sat down at the right hand of
the Majesty on high.

Revelation 5:1-14

[1] Then I saw in the right hand of the one seated on the throne a scroll with writing on both sides, sealed with seven seals. [2] I also saw a mighty angel proclaiming with a loud voice,

"Who is worthy to open the scroll and break its seals?"

[3] But no one in heaven or on earth or under the earth was able to open the scroll or even to look in it. [4] I wept and wept because no one was found worthy to open the scroll or even to look in it. [5] Then one of the elders said to me, "Do not weep. Look, the Lion from the tribe of Judah, the Root of David, has conquered so that he is able to open the scroll and its seven seals."

[6] Then I saw one like a slaughtered lamb standing in the midst of the throne and the four living creatures and among the elders. He had seven horns and seven eyes, which are the seven spirits of God sent into all the earth. [7] He went and took the scroll out of the right hand of the one seated on the throne.

THE LAMB IS WORTHY

[8] When he took the scroll, the four living creatures and the twenty-four elders fell down before the Lamb. Each one had a harp and golden bowls filled with incense, which are the prayers of the saints. [9] And they sang a new song:

> You are worthy to take the scroll
> and to open its seals,
> because you were slaughtered,
> and you purchased people
> for God by your blood
> from every tribe and language
> and people and nation.
> [10] You made them a kingdom
> and priests to our God,
> and they will reign on the earth.

[11] Then I looked and heard the voice of many angels around the throne, and also of the living creatures and of the elders. Their number was countless thousands, plus thousands of thousands. [12] They said with a loud voice,

> Worthy is the Lamb who was slaughtered
> to receive power and riches
> and wisdom and strength
> and honor and glory and blessing!

[13] I heard every creature in heaven, on earth, under the earth, on the sea, and everything in them say,

> Blessing and honor and glory and power
> be to the one seated on the throne,
> and to the Lamb, forever and ever!

[14] The four living creatures said, "Amen," and the elders fell down and worshiped.

DATE

NOTES

DAY

27

Jesus Christ Is Lord

Matthew 11:25-30

THE SON GIVES KNOWLEDGE AND REST

25 At that time Jesus said, "I praise you, Father, Lord of heaven and earth, because you have hidden these things from the wise and intelligent and revealed them to infants. 26 Yes, Father, because this was your good pleasure. 27 All things have been entrusted to me by my Father. No one knows the Son except the Father, and no one knows the Father except the Son and anyone to whom the Son desires to reveal him.

28 "Come to me, all of you who are weary and burdened, and I will give you rest. 29 Take up my yoke and learn from me, because I am lowly and humble in heart, and you will find rest for your souls. 30 For my yoke is easy and my burden is light."

John 3:16

For God loved the world in this way: He gave his one and only Son, so that everyone who believes in him will not perish but have eternal life.

John 6:41-50

⁴¹ Therefore the Jews started complaining about him because he said, "I am the bread that came down from heaven." ⁴² They were saying, "Isn't this Jesus the son of Joseph, whose father and mother we know? How can he now say, 'I have come down from heaven'?"

⁴³ Jesus answered them, "Stop complaining among yourselves. ⁴⁴ No one can come to me unless the Father who sent me draws him, and I will raise him up on the last day. ⁴⁵ It is written in the Prophets: And they will all be taught by God. Everyone who has listened to and learned from the Father comes to me— ⁴⁶ not that anyone has seen the Father except the one who is from God. He has seen the Father.

⁴⁷ "Truly I tell you, anyone who believes has eternal life. ⁴⁸ I am the bread of life. ⁴⁹ Your ancestors ate the manna in the wilderness, and they died. ⁵⁰ This is the bread that comes down from heaven so that anyone may eat of it and not die.

Philippians 2:5-11

⁵ Adopt the same attitude as that of Christ Jesus,

⁶ who, existing in the form of God,
did not consider equality with God
as something to be exploited.

⁷ Instead he emptied himself
by assuming the form of a servant,
taking on the likeness of humanity.

And when he had come as a man,
⁸ he humbled himself by becoming obedient
to the point of death—
even to death on a cross.
⁹ For this reason God highly exalted him
and gave him the name
that is above every name,
¹⁰ so that at the name of Jesus
every knee will bow—
in heaven and on earth
and under the earth—
¹¹ and every tongue will confess
that Jesus Christ is Lord,
to the glory of God the Father.

DATE

NOTES

Natalie's Caramel Corn

BY RAECHEL MYERS AND NATALIE GRANT

SERVES: 4-8 (OR JUST 1)

My friend Natalie is a fair weather hockey fan, but year-round caramel corn fan. The last time her family came over to watch a hockey game, Natalie brought "the world's best caramel corn" for us to munch on between fights and icing calls. I don't remember much about who won the game that night, but the memory of that caramel corn is clear as day. A year-round win, caramel corn is especially appropriate for the holidays. Make a batch to keep on-hand for drop-in holiday guests or that last-minute party invite. Just don't make it too early, or you may not have any left to share.

INGREDIENTS

2 bags buttered
microwave popcorn

1 cup butter

1 cup white sugar

1/3 cup water

DIRECTIONS

Prepare microwave popcorn as directed and set aside. Try your best to remove any unpopped kernels.

Combine butter, sugar, and water in a saucepan. Cook on high, stirring constantly.

Once it reaches a steady boil, decrease heat to medium, continuing to stir until it reaches a good caramel brown color. Plan on 15-20 minutes of stirring. When you think it's done, stir it 5 more seconds, then it's ready.

Pour the hot caramel over the popcorn and stir to evenly coat. Be careful—it's very hot!

Let sit 5 minutes, then serve.

D A T E

Grace Day

Advent is a season of anticipation and celebration. We long for the promised Savior's return, even as we rejoice that He has already come to us. Use this day to pause and reflect on this verse from Galatians, which reminds us why Jesus was born.

When the time
came to completion,
God sent his Son,
born of a woman,
born under the law,
to redeem those under
the law, so that we
might receive adoption
as sons.

GALATIANS 4:4-5

And HEAVEN and NATURE Sing

A Prayer for the First Sunday After Christmas Day

Almighty God, you have poured upon us the new light of your incarnate Word: Grant that this light, enkindled in our hearts, may shine forth in our lives; through Jesus Christ our Lord, who lives and reigns with you, in the unity of the Holy Spirit, one God, now and forever. Amen.

from *The Book of Common Prayer*

SCRIPTURE

John 8:12

Jesus spoke to them again: "I am the light of the world. Anyone who follows me will never walk in the darkness but will have the light of life."

Christmas Cross Stitch

WHAT YOU'LL NEED

Size 24 tapestry needle

Size 14 cross stitch fabric (white or ivory)

DMC embroidery floss in green (500), pink (353), and red (349)

Embroidery hoop (9" works well for this project)

Scissors

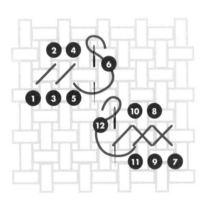

Share your progress using #SheReadsTruth or by tagging @shereadstruth on social media.

TO BEGIN

Find the center of the pattern (marked) and the center of your fabric. This is where you'll begin stitching. Now, center fabric in the embroidery hoop, and secure.

Because you'll begin with the holly leaf, start with your green floss. Cut a piece of floss the length of your arm, separate out 2 of the 6 threads, then thread them through your needle. Set the remaining 4 threads aside to use as you need them, 2 at a time.

To begin stitching, bring the threaded needle up from the back of the fabric, leaving a tail of about an inch of floss behind the fabric. Stitch the next 3 or 4 stitches over the tail. Clip off the extra thread.

STITCHING

There are two methods. The first method is to work a row of half stitches / / / / , then work back \ \ \ \ to complete the X's (see illustration). Use this method for most stitching. The second method is to complete each X as you go. Use this method for vertical rows of stitches.

The sign of a real cross stitch pro is when all of the X's are crossed in the same direction (that is, the top thread of the X always slants in the same direction, either \ or /). If you're a beginner, don't worry about this little detail. But if you're up for the challenge, give it a try!

FINISHING

When you come to the end of a thread, or to change to a new color, use your needle to weave the thread through the last 5 or 6 stitches on the back side of your fabric. Clip the thread short so as not to leave a loose tail. Then start your next color or another thread of the same color with the next stitch, securing the tail as you did before.

When your project is complete, remove it from the hoop. Before you display your work, smooth it and remove wrinkles by placing another cloth on top of the needlework and pressing lightly with a warm iron.

Display your finished creation in a frame or in an embroidery hoop.

The Lord has done great things for us; we are glad. - Psalm 126:3 ESV

Where did I spend Christmas Day?

_____

WHAT TIME DID I WAKE UP?

AM

PM

WHAT WAS THE WEATHER LIKE?

(circle one)

HIGH

LOW

Who did I celebrate Christmas with?

WHAT DID WE EAT?

WHAT MADE US LAUGH?

WHAT TRADITION MEANT THE MOST TO ME THIS YEAR?

What Christmas song did I play the most this Advent season?

TITLE: _____

ARTIST: _____

I LOVED GIVING THIS GIFT

GIFT: _____

TO: _____

GIFT: _____

FROM: _____

I LOVED RECEIVING THIS GIFT

MY FAVORITE ADVENT SCRIPTURE:

MY PRAYER FOR THE COMING YEAR:

END DATE

MONTH   DAY   YEAR

13 JESUS WASHES HIS DISCIPLES' FEET

It was just before the Passover Festival. Jesus knew that his hour had come for him to leave this world and go to the Father. Having loved his own who were in the world, he loved them to the end.

The evening meal was in progress, and the devil had already prompted Judas, the son of Simon Iscariot, to betray Jesus. Jesus knew that the Father had put all things under his power, and that he had come from God and was returning to God; so he got up from the meal, took off his outer clothing, and wrapped a towel around his waist. After that, he poured water into a basin and began to wash his disciples' feet, drying them with the towel that was wrapped around him.

He came to Simon Peter, who said to him, "Lord, are you going to wash my feet?"

Jesus replied, "You do not realize now what I am doing, but later you will understand."

"No," said Peter, "you shall never wash my feet."

Jesus answered, "Unless I wash you, you have no part with me."

"Then, Lord," Simon Peter replied, "not just my feet but my hands and my head as well!"

Jesus answered, "Those who have had a bath need only to wash their feet; their whole body is clean. And you are clean, though not every one of you." For he knew who was going to betray him, and that was why he said not every one was clean.

THE MEANING OF FOOT WASHING

When he had finished washing their feet, he put on his clothes and returned to his place. "Do you understand what I have done for you?" he asked them. "You call me 'Teacher' and 'Lord,' and rightly so, for that is what I am. Now that I, your Lord and Teacher, have washed your feet, you also should wash one another's feet. I have set you an example that you should do as I have done for you. Very truly I tell you, no servant is greater than his master, nor is a messenger greater than the one who sent him. Now that you know these things, you will be blessed if you do them.

"I am not referring to all of you; I know those I have chosen. But this is to fulfill this passage of Scripture: 'He who shared my bread has turned against me.'

"I am telling you now before it happens, so that when it does happen you will believe that I am who I am. Very truly I tell you, whoever accepts anyone I send accepts me; and whoever accepts me accepts the one who sent me."

JUDAS'S BETRAYAL PREDICTED

After he had said this, Jesus was troubled in spirit and testified, "Very truly I tell you, one of you is going to betray me."

His disciples stared at one another, at a loss to know which of them he meant.

a 13:18 Psalm 41:9

823

He is the trouble of salt

He never stopped teaching

He never stopped serving

824

A Bible that feels like home.

The *She Reads Truth Bible* is designed with you in mind—to invite you to count yourself among the She Reads Truth community of "Women in the Word of God every day." This Bible features introductions and Scripture reading plans for each book of the Bible, with supplemental passages for deeper understanding; 66 carefully selected and artfully designed key verses; full-color maps, charts, and timelines; devotionals by the She Reads Truth writing team; wide margins for journaling and note-taking, and more.

**This is not a Bible for your shelf.
It is a Bible for your life.**

SHE READS TRUTH | BIBLE

BIBLIOGRAPHY

Collins, Ace. *Stories Behind the Great Traditions of Christmas.* Grand Rapids, MI: Zondervan, 2003.

Editorial. "Lego in Numbers." *The Telegraph.* August 30, 2011. http://www.telegraph.co.uk/finance/
newsbysector/retailandconsumer/8360246/Lego-in-numbers.html

Gulevich, Tanya. *Encyclopedia of Christmas.* Detroit, MI: Omnigraphics, Inc., 2000.

Grant, George and Gregory Wilbur. *Christmas Spirit: The Joyous Stories, Carols, Feasts, and Traditions of the
Season.* Nashville: Cumberland House, 1999.

Green, Jonathan. *Christmas Miscellany: Everything You Always Wanted to Know About Christmas.* Brattleboro,
VT: Skyhorse Publishing, Inc., 2009.

"Rosemary and Garlic Roast Beef" adapted from oliviascuisine.com.

SUBSCRIPTION INQUIRIES

orders@shereadstruth.com

COLOPHON

This book was printed offset in Nashville, Tennessee, on 70# Lynx Opaque. Typefaces used include Futura,
Garamond, and Salome. Cover is printed offset on Royal Sundance Linen Emerald Green 100C with gold
and white foil. Insert paper is Neenah: Eames White 50T Diffused; Architecture. Finished size is 8"x10".

EDITORIAL

EDITORS-IN-CHIEF

Raechel Myers and Amanda Bible Williams

CONTENT DIRECTOR

Russ Ramsey, MDiv., ThM.

MANAGING EDITOR

Jessica Lamb

EDITOR

Kara Gause

EDITORIAL ASSISTANT

Ellen Taylor

ADDITIONAL THEOLOGICAL OVERSIGHT

Nate Shurden, MDiv.

CREATIVE

CREATIVE DIRECTOR

Ryan Myers

ART DIRECTOR

Amanda Barnhart

DESIGNER

Kelsea Allen

PHOTOGRAPHER

Abigail Bobo

LETTERING ARTIST

Eva Winters

FOLIAGE ILLUSTRATIONS

Shealeen Louise

STOP BY

shereadstruth.com

SHOP

shopshereadstruth.com

KEEP IN TOUCH

@shereadstruth

DOWNLOAD THE APP

SEND A NOTE

hello@shereadstruth.com

CONNECT

#SheReadsTruth

She Reads Truth is a worldwide community of women who read God's Word together every day.

Founded in 2012, She Reads Truth invites women of all ages to engage with Scripture through daily reading plans, online conversation led by a vibrant community of contributors, and offline resources created at the intersection of beauty, goodness, and Truth.

These Scripture memory cards
correspond to the Sundays of Advent
in the **Joy to the World: Advent 2017**
reading plan.

Punch out the cards and carry them
with you, place them where you'll see
them often, or share them with a friend.

And as a bonus, our little Christmas
present to you: four gift tags for tying
onto packages!